Short Scenes for Auditions and Acting Class

Frank Catalano

Lexington Avenue Press
Copyright © 2017 Frank Catalano
All rights reserved.
ISBN-10: 1535149310
ISBN-13: 9781535149310

Short Scenes for Auditions

and Acting Class

TABLE OF CONTENTS

Introduction 1

What Is A Scene? 5

    A scene is something seen by a viewer or prospect: 6

    A scene is the place where an action or event occurs: 6

    A scene is the place in which the action of a play,
    movie or other narrative occurs: 6

    A scene is a subdivision of an act in a dramatic presentation
    in which the setting is fixed and the time continuous: 7

    A scene is a shot or series of shots in a movie constituting
    a unit of continuous related action: 7

Point Of View – What's The Idea Behind A Scene? 9

Why Do I Have To Do A Scene? 13

How Do I Select A Scene That's Right For Me? 15

    By Casting Type 15

    To showcase talent or skills 15

    Compatibility with career and artistic goals 16

What About Performing My Scene? 17

    Creating character attributes 17

    Intellectual: 18

    Emotional: 18

Physical: 19

Spiritual: 19

What's The Best Way To Memorize My Lines And Create A Physical Life For My Character? 22

Creating An Implementation Strategy That Works 24

What is An Implementation 24

Creating A Performance Dynamic – How To Make A Creative Box To Play In 25

Using "What If?" 27

Creating The "Moment Before." 29

Creating "Now" Using Objectives And Beats 30

What is your character's main objective? 30

What are your character's sub-objectives?
Mark them as individual beats. 30

What are the obstacles in the way of achieving your objectives? 32

What is going on NOW on at this moment? 32

When is this moment in time? 33

Where are you? What is the space your character lives in? 33

Creating The "Moment After." 34

Where are you going? 34

Everyone likes to know where they have been and where they are going. 34

    How do you play the moment after? 35

    How do you show the moment after? 35

How Do I Begin A Scene At An Acting Class Or Audition? 36

Where Should I Look When I Perform A Scene For An
Acting Class Or Audition? 39

How Do I End My Scene At An Acting Class Or Audition? 41

How Do I Select A Scene Partner For An Acting Class
Assignment Or Audition? 43

    Character type 43

    Talent, skills and commitment 44

    Dating? 45

How Do I Rehearse A Scene For An Acting Class Or Audition? 46

What If The Script Is Too Long Or Too Short? 48

Presenting - In Class Versus For An Audition 49

    Creating a point of view: 49

    Experimentation during rehearsal – try new things but
    then make specific choices 49

Creating An Interesting Character 51

    Creating a Character 51

    Reading the Script 51

Setting Objectives For Your Character 53

Macro: Create an objective for the entire piece..................................53

Micro: Create Objectives for each scene 53

Obstacles 54

Create an objective from your own interpretation 55

How To Have Fun At An Acting Class Or Audition................................57

How To Use This Book..59

THE SCENES

#1	THE HIT	MALE/MALE	COMEDY	63
#2	AMERICA	MALE/FEMALE	DRAMA	69
#3	THE FORTUNE TELLER	MALE/FEMALE	COMEDY	75
#4	GODS AND MONSTERS	MALE/MALE	DRAMA	83
#5	LOOKING	MALE/FEMALE	DRAMA	91
#6	DANTE AND THE WAITER	MALE/FEMALE	DRAMA	97
#7	MEMORY LANE	MALE/FEMALE	DRAMA/COMEDY	105
#8	YOU NEVER TELL ME YOU LOVE ME	MALE/FEMALE	COMEDY	113
#9	BERLIN – DECEMBER 1941	MALE/FEMALE	DRAMA	121
#10	SHAKESPEARE	MALE/FEMALE	COMEDY	127
#11	HOT TUB CONFESSION	MALE/FEMALE	DRAMA/COMEDY	133
#12	THE FABULOUS JOHNNY ANGEL	MALE/FEMALE	DRAMA/COMEDY	141
#13	THE GOOD SAMARITAN	MALE/MALE	DRAMA	149
#14	THE LIBRARY	FEMALE/FEMALE	COMEDY	157
#15	HAUNTED	FEMALE/MALE	DRAMA	163
#16	HOME SWEET HOME	MALE/FEMALE	COMEDY	171

#17 THE HAPPY HOUR	MALE/FEMALE	COMEDY	 179
#18 THE SPLIT	MALE/FEMALE	COMEDY	 187
#19 THE WINDOW JOB	MALE/FEMALE	COMEDY	 193
#20 THE END	MALE/MALE	COMEDY	 199
#21 CHE CHE – THE SONG	MALE/FEMALE	DRAMA	 209
#22 CHE CHE – COFFEE	MALE/FEMALE	DRAMA	 213
#23 AUTUMN SWEET AUTUMN 1989 – THE FIRST DAY – SABRINA, SCRAMBLED EGGS AND THE LETTERS	MALE/FEMALE	DRAMA	 219
#24 AUTUMN SWEET AUTUMN 1989 – THE SECOND DAY – CHIAROSCURO, LIPTON TEA, AND THE PAINT BOX	MALE/FEMALE	DRAMA	 225
#25 THE SIGHTING	MALE/FEMALE	DRAMA	 233

Introduction

As an author, I have written several monologue books including ***ART OF THE MONOLGUE, WHITE KNIGHT BLACK NIGHT*** and ***SHORT MONOLOGUES FOR AUDITIONS*** – which concentrated upon the performance of theatrical monologues as a creative artistic work, in acting classes and auditions. This current volume will focus upon the presentation of two character scenes for the purpose of auditions or as creative learning tools in an acting class. Most auditions you will have in your career will require you to "cold read" from the specific script or part you are being considered for. However, you will also encounter auditions for agents, casting directors, directors of acting companies or conservatory schools, where they will ask you to bring in a scene with another actor. I will explore in detail how to prepare and present such material in all situations.

As in the monologue books, I will show you how to focus on the selection and presentation of the material to fit within your abilities to convey them in an audition or class setting. Why short scenes? As an acting teacher, I have always advised my students **"*less is more.*"** You should not have to prepare and perform a twenty-minute scene for an audition or acting teacher to get an idea of what your talent might be. Whether auditioning or in an acting class, you will learn how to showcase a certain aspect of your talent, physicality and demonstrate an understanding of the material for a certain role. You will also learn how to create specific goals for different settings. For example, for an acting class, the goal might be to provide the teacher a sample of your acting abilities, your demeanor, ability to take direction and ultimately to determine what areas of your performing skills you might need to work on. In an audition for an agent or casting director, they may want to see how you perform prepared material to access how you might fit into their client list or project. The same criteria might apply to a director of a theatre company or a university theatre conservatory school audition. Of course, are looking for a specific type to fit into their company or school. But they also want to see how you take prepared material and create the moment on your own. Auditions in any setting are exhibitions in samples. You must create a "sample" of who you are and what you can do. A whole performance is not needed. Think of it as a small taste of the chef's dish... not the whole meal. What about material?

All actors, if they work on stage, film and television, should have at least two short contemporary scenes (one comedy and one dramatic) ready to go at all times. If you are applying to a conservatory school, you should also add to that at least one classical scene to your acting arsenal. Note, some schools may require you to select material from a specific list from plays while others will let you bring in material of your choice. If you prepare, well-known material from familiar sources, most acting teachers and auditioners will have seen other actors perform the same material. Here, you run the danger of comparison. As you perform they will be thinking about the last person that presented the same material. How did they do it? How does your interpretation differ? Which one of you is better? In a class setting, when you present a scene in front of the class, you are creating a presentation within a small controlled universe. You don't want class members or acting teacher to compare you with anyone else within that controlled universe. You want the presentation to be only about you. This is not about being selfish or non supportive. You want your acting teacher and fellow class members to know you for who **you** are instead of experiencing you through the filter of someone else. A professional presentation can establish your ranking within that small universe. You can be the "sought after performer" that everyone wants to work with or the "the wall flower" who rarely gets an opportunity to work. Acting classes can be exciting or a dull experience if you are relegated to being a watcher not a doer. What kind of material is contained in this book?

The scenes contained within this book are designed to be general enough so that you can layer in those elements of your talent that you want to showcase. In addition, it will pair your character with an entirely different character so that a scene partner will add to and not compete with what you are trying to create. This book will also show you how to make a selection of material that fits **only you**. You will create scenes that agents, casting directors, acting teachers and classmates can only imagine you performing and showing how you connect to an audience emotionally, intellectually and physically. Generally, how long are the scenes in this book?

Remember, **less is more**. Most scenes are one to two minutes in length and will act as a sample of what you can do, not the whole performance. If you are auditioning, this is a showcase of your talent. If you are presenting this in a class, it is also a showcase of your talent but also an indicator of what you might need to work on. You might be thinking, how will I learn anything new if I am showcasing what I do best? The answer, it can give your acting teacher an idea of what doesn't need to be expanded, so he/she can focus on other areas. You will lead with strengths and then build upon that with the help of your acting teacher. For example, if you have difficulty showing emotion, please don't lead with an emotional scene. Select something that showcases your physicality or intellectual approach to language or theme. Yes, it's an acting class, but it's just like an audition because you are being evaluated. Don't ever forget that you are operating in a small controlled universe and that your standing in such universe is subject to fluctuate just like a stock in the New York Stock Exchange. Some students consistently bring in well-prepared and exceptional material and immediately get the respect of the acting teacher and other students. However, that respect may change as future work presents itself or (perhaps worse) that exceptional student does the same material over an over again.

I had a short-lived membership in a Los Angeles based theatre company several years ago. It was a "working company" which meant most of its members were recognizable working actors. There were workshops and classes along with performing as part of the ensemble. I was invited to become a member (which required dues) and attended an introductory presentation. I thought the work presented by more than a few famous theatre actors was excellent. I immediately joined and paid the dues and attended workshops and presentations throughout the next year. From that point on, everything I saw or attended was the exact same performance and material I saw the first time. There was no growth at all. The final nail in the coffin for me was I attended the "new" introductory presentation a full year later... and what I saw was exactly the same. My conclusion was this company was more like a museum than a vibrant creative group of actors. I quit and never looked back. I have gone off track to make a point. Always lead with your strongest abilities so that you establish a base line within the acting class. After that, don't be afraid to add to that baseline by trying new things. Some will not work well when you start off, but then you will get stronger as you move forward.

This book contains twenty-five original two-person scenes that can be performed by male or female characters. Each scene will be prefaced with the following information:

Title:

Gender: (Male/Female)

Age Range: (Including gender)

Characters: (Description)

Location: (Where the scene takes place)

Time: (When the scene takes place)

Synopsis (A general description of what happens)

Genre: (Comedy or Drama)

There is an equal mix of comedy and drama and all are within the one to two minute time range. Think about who your scene partner will be and then find a scene that you both can closely connect to either on an emotional or intellectual level. Ultimately, the right scene for you and your scene partner is one that showcases both of your unique talents. Think of an audition scene as a means to end. As an audition piece, it's going to exhibit what you both can do. If it is a class assignment, let it provide an acting teacher a specific insight about who you are, your talents and what areas of acting you need to work on. We will discuss the selection of a scene partner later in this book.

Lastly, scenes are subject to our tastes and needs at any given moment. Don't be afraid to try many different scenes from this book as your creative growth progresses or you feel you need to do something different. Make this book your source for the magic that you will do. Go back to it again and again whenever you feel there is a need for it.

What Is A Scene?

I think it's important to understand exactly what you are presenting when you select material to perform. The minimal answer is that a scene is a set number of pages from a play or film script that contain ACTION, DESCRIPTION and DIALOGUE. Also that within those set number of pages, actors must establish a WHO, WHAT, WHERE, WHEN and WHY reality for the characters and actions contained in them. Students often bring scenes into my classes that fail to establish even a few of the criteria that we have established above. They often have the characters down and the characters speak, but there is no reason for them to speak or do anything for that matter. So, become talking heads struggling in a vacuum because they have nothing to act. When I ask them why their character did what he/she did? They reply, "**Because that's the way it was in the movie."** They operate at a disadvantage if that is the criteria they have chosen. Whatever they have seen from a movie has been edited with music and effects added and are quite a different performance dynamic that presenting in an audition or class. When they use a movie or a clip from YouTube as a reference that do not take into consideration that one scene which appears in a movie may be a small fragment of a larger scene. The students present the fragment as a stand alone in class and it may only run forty-five seconds and nothing happens. Why? It is incomplete. If you do a fragment of a scene as part of audition sides in a cold reading, the casting director has selected the material for very specific reasons, which may not require a whole interpretation. However as an actor, even when presenting a scene, you should have an idea of how the part you are performing relates to the whole. It might mean reading the entire script in order to give meaning to the two-minute scene you are performing. A producer once wanted to know if I ever dipped a piece of bread in a cooking pot of tomato sauce. I wasn't sure if I did or not but I said told him I did. Then he smiled and said, if you stir the pot, and take a small taste, shouldn't it be representative of the whole pot? I'm getting hungry writing this, but you get my message. The scene, even though a small taste must be representative of the entire work. Let's look at what a scene actually can be so that you can know what to act and how to put it together for an audition or an acting class. The American Heritage Dictionary definition states:

A SCENE IS SOMETHING SEEN BY A VIEWER OR PROSPECT:

This is often forgotten when a scene is presented. Actors have the tendency to focus inwardly toward their character and forget that they are presenting material for an audience. Always ask yourself, where is the audience and how can I frame the situation and action so that they can be involved in it intellectually and emotionally?

A SCENE IS THE PLACE WHERE AN ACTION OR EVENT OCCURS:

When creating the reality of the moment in a scene don't forget to also establish the universe that your character is living within. Your character will have to react to that universe and it influence the "how" and "why" they do what they do within the scene.

A SCENE IS THE PLACE IN WHICH THE ACTION OF A PLAY, MOVIE OR OTHER NARRATIVE OCCURS:

This is the literal location. The house, the living room, the study etc.... but it is so much more. It's not just about the literal location or setting of the action. What is specific about the space? What is its ownership? If you were to set a scene in the middle of the night at a graveyard – that would be one location. But what if you were to set a scene in the middle of the night at a graveyard, standing over a grave with your character's name on it. Is the grave empty or does it have someone in it? If so, who? This location would change the emotional center of a character within a scene. The place can also be somewhere other than the literal location of the character within a scene. In Anton Chekov's play THREE SISTERS, Irina Sergeyevna Prozorova, the youngest of the three, longs to go to Moscow. Although the actual location of the play is not in Moscow, Irina's hopes and dreams all live there. This is where she emanates from. So a place within a scene can be many things.

A SCENE IS A SUBDIVISION OF AN ACT IN A DRAMATIC PRESENTATION IN WHICH THE SETTING IS FIXED AND THE TIME CONTINUOUS:

A scene, if it is part of a play, is like one tile of a mosaic. It has it's own beginning, middle and end which is connected to a larger narrative. When you perform a scene, even if it is a stand alone, you must incorporate the reality of the larger narrative. It doesn't mean you have to play, as I stated earlier, the whole play, but you must take into account where the scene that you are performing falls within the larger context. We will talk more about this when I discuss the moment before, now and the moment after. Consider as the scene begins, what moment or event has triggered initial the moment you are playing at the start of your action.

A SCENE IS A SHOT OR SERIES OF SHOTS IN A MOVIE CONS-TITUTING A UNIT OF CONTINUOUS RELATED ACTION:

In film, the location can change so the setting is not fixed. Also film is usually shot out of order, so while the same theory applies pertaining to a linear narrative, film is more visual and move back and forth within time frames and action. You still have to play the larger narrative, however you need to be aware of how and in what order that narrative is written in the body of the screenplay.

So performing a scene is a lot more than just two characters facing each other and talking. It is also, a bit more than simply playing who, what, when, where and why? You really have to look at the whole piece that the scene emanates from to truly understand then convey the "why."

Before we leave this section of the book I want to say a few words about monologues as they appear within a scene. By definition, a monologue as a long speech made by one person, often monopolizing a conversation. You may be thinking, I already know that, tell me something I don't know. Okay, a monologue can also be part of a scene or treated as a scene when performed. When monologues are performed they are almost always performed with one person on the stage or within a camera shot speaking. That's how a monologue is usually presented as part of an audition. However, when presented within the body of a work (a play or film) a monologue could be lines spoken by one character to other characters, inanimate objects or animals. An example is the play or film WAR HORSE (2011). Throughout the play and film, there are characters that speak alone (monologue) to the horse. When the words are spoken and there is a reaction, a monologue is really a scene. The words spoken should be such that they have depth and special meaning. Unless, you count as a monologue leaving phone message, placing an order at the automated machine at Jack in the Box or trying to talk on the phone to customer service at a bank, monologues should be treated as a scene. Now that we have an idea of what a scene is, lets take a look at the way to prepare a scene for presentation.

Point Of View – What's The Idea Behind A Scene?

All actors should also be producers. What do producers do? Aside from the common belief that they provide the funding for a presentation, they also are often the creative force behind it. They take the idea along with the help of a director and develop it into a tangible presentation. When you prepare a scene for an audition or acting class, you must consider how it will be presented. It may be a much smaller scale, but the process should be no different than producing the entire work for an audience. I'm not suggesting that you go crazy with special effects, scenery and extravagant costume. But I am suggesting that you consider how you will present the scene to an audience and what you will contribute to that end. I probably shouldn't talk about sports because I know very little. But think for a moment about a baseball player at bat. He or she is playing within a baseball game in which the overall goal is for his or her team to win. That's one part and then the next question is how at that very moment at bat does that player fit into the overall scenario. You might say that's easy hit the ball as hard and as far as you can. Get a home run! But that might not be it. The coach may have that batter bunt to load the bases and bring in a heavy hitter to hit the home run. Preparing a scene is no different, you must consider what is the overall goal of your presentation and how do you fit and serve that goal. Notice, I'm not talking about character motivation, I'm talking about creating a ***point of view*** that focuses the framework of ***how*** the scene will be presented and in what context.

Don't fall into the trap that an outlandish interpretation of the role focusing solely your acting ability alone to deliver it is all that is needed to connect to an audience. Yes, it is true that as an actor, it's what you bring to the script and that is why we experience different actors portrayals of the same roles. We see the same plays again and again, not for the story as much as for the interpretation of the actor playing the role. But a scene presentation should not only be about your performance. It should be about your performance presented within a specific point of view. The presentation of any scene must have a creative framework or point of view. Many acting teachers may talk to you about making choices for your character. What I am talking about is creating a structure and making choices that concern the framework that your character can play within. Once the structure is created, then you can make individual acting choices and immerse yourself within those your character. Let's think of it this way. It's as if you build a wooden box and that box is your framework. Once established, you can then get as crazy as you want as long as that box remains together. If it falls apart, everything else within the scene will fall apart as well. What does a framework or point of view for a scene actually consist of?

First of all, you should set goals (not only for your character) but for the scene as a whole. What do you want to accomplish when this scene is presented to an audience? Do you want the audience to a have a certain emotional experience or intellectual reaction to your presentation? What if you don't have point of view for a framework? This is what rehearsal is for, to experiment to see what works and what does not. Always remember, the creative process is often long and filled with disappointment. Most of your ideas WILL NOT work. Think about Thomas Edison's quote about how many failed ideas he went through to invent the electric light bulb. **"I have not failed. I've just found 10,000 ways that won't work."** Creating a framework and point of view for a scene is not inventing a light bulb, but the creative process is the same. Once you have achieved a basic foundation, you will have gone a long way to understanding what internal choices you will need to portray your character to an audience. Never forget, just because you created it doesn't mean that it is the best choice. Consider how your choices will work with a particular audience. Sometimes what seems like a great idea in rehearsal will be a disaster in performance. Let look at an example.

Several years ago, I attended a production of William Shakespeare's Hamlet at small theatre in Los Angeles. I sat in the first row about three feet from the actor who played Hamlet as he uttered those famous lines **"To be or not to be..."** I had experienced this soliloquy dozens of times before within a representational framework where the Hamlet character reveals his inner thoughts by speaking to himself aloud. In this particular production, and without warning, the actor who played Hamlet turned toward only toward me and asked the famous question, **"To be or not to be?"** At first I wanted to blurt out like Robert Di Niro in **Taxi Driver, "Are you talking to me?"** But, somehow thought it might not be appropriate. The audience, all eyes on me, waited for me to reply. At first I said nothing. But, to be polite, I decided to give him a look of acknowledgment. As if to say **"I heard that… and that is definitely a question to consider."** Once that choice was made, a performance dynamic had been established and like a bell once rung, it could not be undone. For the rest of the show, every time a line was emphasized or thought spoken, the audience turned toward me for a reaction. I never gave one. I am not saying that it was wrong to present the Hamlet soliloquy in this manner. Someone in the production made a choice to do it that way. The creative framework of that particular production of Hamlet was centered on Hamlet acknowledging the presence of one member of the audience. At that particular performance, I unwittingly assumed that role. I could have chosen to respond verbally to Hamlet, but I chose just to nod at him to acknowledge his line to me. However, we can say that Hamlet acknowledging one member of the audience in the middle of his soliloquy was done for a special reason. Perhaps to emphasize the torment of Hamlet's character and may have been a great idea when first brought up in rehearsal. However, I don't think there was much consideration of how this idea would influence an audience experiencing the work. I am assuming that the source of the creative framework of this production of Hamlet would rest with the production's director.

The Director of Hamlet created a point of view or framework to present Shakespeare's play that allowed for the acknowledgment of a single member of the audience when Hamlet reveals his inner most thoughts… namely his soliloquies. Just in case you forgot, a soliloquy is when a character speaks their inner thoughts out loud. They are often highly personal and reveal some inner workings of the characters psyche. So, when I was chosen at random or because I was seated in a specific place to be the receiver of such inner thought, it immediately thrust me into the play and set me aside from the rest of the audience. Setting up a soliloquy in this way elevated my presence and made me sort of a confidant to Hamlet's inner thoughts. The problem was that I was not a confidant and didn't have the opportunity to respond. Shakespeare had not written any lines for me... and I would not presume that the director wanted me to go off in iambic pentameter. So I sat and listened to him and became a sort of distraction for the rest of the play. Every time I moved, the audience would turn and look at me. I remember having to scratch my nose but didn't because I was afraid of how it might be interpreted. So, what might have been a great idea in rehearsal turned out to be a very bad idea in presentation.

When you choose to perform a particular scene, just like a producer or director, you must choose **how** you will convey the reality of your character within a particular situation to an audience. Every scene needs an idea behind it. You should have a clear idea of its point of view when you present this material and what is the desired outcome? Also, remember to make choices that work for your goals. For example, in an audition or class I think it is best to create a framework that does not acknowledge the auditioner or acting teacher. This allows them the freedom to make notes on your performance, sit back and see what you can do. You don't want them; feeling forced to react to a gaze or directed line toward them. It will make them uncomfortable and lessen your chance to showcase what you can do. Your creative framework in presenting a scene should be focused on how to best present the reality of the characters you have created and to connect those characters with your talents. The purpose of an audition scene or class scene is not to solely entertain, it is to show how you create a characters and the universe they live in, interpret their dialogue and physicality to an audience.

Now that we have discussed what a scene is and how it should be presented, let's get back to our original question. Why do we have to do scenes for auditions and classes anyway?

Why Do I Have To Do A Scene?

A lot of students will ask me why they have to do scenes in an acting class and that they would rather get up and perform improvisations. An improvised scene has many of the qualities of a written scene and can demonstrate an actor's ability to showcase their talents. So why bother having to prepare a memorized a scene? Also, scenes usually aren't used for the actual casting of roles in a play or film. Most casting directors, when reading actors for a particular project, like to have the work performed from sides of a specific script they are casting either as a cold reading or a memorized screen test. So having one or more scenes prepared is not going to land you a specific role in a film or television program. In order to do that, you are going to have to do a **cold reading** of the specific material from the project. The old school definition of a **cold reading** is when an actor auditioning for a particular role performs from part of a script or other text with little or no rehearsal, practice or study in advance. However, modern technology and the Internet makes almost all audition material available in advance. Actors can purchase these materials for a small fee or if they have representation, the agency will provide it to them in an email in advance. So, cold readings are rarely really cold. Most sides are downloaded and memorized before the audition. If you cannot use a prepared scene for a stage, film or television audition, why bother working on one?

The answer to the question of why we do prepared scenes for acting classes and auditions is to be able to show an acting teacher, casting director, agent or performing arts school representative our ability to perform prepared (rather than cold) material. In this book, I have developed primarily shorter scenes that run approximately two minutes specifically for auditions and acting classes. As an audition piece, an actor wants to present a scene work that is a concise sample of his/her work which highlights their ability to memorize dialogue, create the intellectual, emotional, physical and spiritual state of a character. It should also exhibit an actor's creative ability to present prepared material from a specific point of view. In a classroom/studio setting, an actor can work on specific challenges of character creation, line memorization, nervousness and physicality. The "how" and "why" we do scenes then is clear. This is a sample of how you can interpret material when you have had a time to prepare it and present it within a specific creative framework. However, just because it is prepared, you are not expected to create a whole play. What is expected is for you to provide a short sample (one to two minutes) of your creativity and talent to a specific audience. Who is this audience? It can be an acting teacher, an acting class, an agent, and a producer, casting director, an artistic director of a theatre ensemble, and an admissions committee at an acting school/college or a director of a play or film. However, the **who** is not as important as the **how** you create it. The first step in this process is the selection of the right material.

How Do I Select A Scene That's Right For Me?

BY CASTING TYPE

No matter how versatile you think you may be as a performer, an acting teacher, a casting director or agent will only see you playing roles that they feel fall within your appropriate casting type. Your **casting type** is a combination of factors which can include age, physical stature, ethnicity, the way you speak, demeanor and generally the way you appear to most people most of the time. You want to select a scene that is **type appropriate** for you. That is, if you are female age twenties, you should not select a character that is an older woman in her fifties. But now you are thinking I am an actor I should be able to portray any person or age. True, but your casting type is centered on who you really are so select a scene to play a character that is generally your own age. Acting teachers, agents and casting directors will look to identify you in one type category or another and there is not much you can do about that.

TO SHOWCASE TALENT OR SKILLS

If you are preparing a scene for an acting class or for an audition you want to select material that will highlight the talent and skills that you do the best. If you have difficulty in showing intense emotion, then stay away from those types of scenes until you can perfect the skill to perform them. Work with a scene partner to select a scene that will highlight what you do best. If you are doing a short scene as an audition for an agent, select something contemporary no longer than two minutes. I say contemporary unless you are auditioning for a classical theatre company. If not, then try to select material that showcases your specific talents and is appropriate for your casting type and representative of what you would be submitted for by that agent. If you feel your strongest talent is comedy, then lead with that. If you feel your strongest talent is drama, then lead with that.

COMPATIBILITY WITH CAREER AND ARTISTIC GOALS

Select scenes that are compatible with the creative goals you are attempting to achieve. If you are auditioning for a commercial agent, a crisp, short, high-energy (but not too happy) scene would probably be best. A longer dramatic narrative or verse scene would not be the best choice for a commercial agent, but may work in perfectly for an audition for a theatrical agent for film and television representation or an audition for membership into a theatre company.

Also, an acting teacher may ask you to select a scene from a play or film so that you can work on a specific acting goal such as anger, physicality or listening. For example, if you are asked to work on a specific emotion, select a scene that will stretch your abilities in that area.

What About Performing My Scene?

What are some considerations I should think about when performing a scene for an acting class or audition?

CREATING CHARACTER ATTRIBUTES

Many actors hate performing memorized scenes because they absolutely hate trying to memorize lines and feel scenes are not a true representation of their acting ability. Actors become obsessed with learning every coma and word of the script they are attempting to perform or they abandon the script all together. This is often the result of not enough rehearsal time or no rehearsal at all. I can't count the number of times an actor who couldn't remember his/her lines told me that they knew every word by heart when the did it in their car. What's wrong with that? They may have run lines perfectly in their car but they were training their brain to key in certain lines to the physical activity of driving instead of connecting to the reality of their scene.

Many actors believe that performing in a prepared scene is too restrictive and does not provide the opportunity to show a casting director or agent the full range of an actor's ability to truly react to another character. They feel it is an artificial situation set in a limited environment (in an office or on a bare stage) where both actors in the scene try to showcase their talents and do not much more. Many actors literally fall into the trap of performing a recitation of the lines from cue to cue. What is a cue? A cue is the verbal or physical trigger for an action to be carried out or a line spoken within a script. So many actors in a class or audition situation just recite their lines from cue to cue without much feeling or thought of what is really going on. At other times actors performing in scenes feel they have to embellish each moment with long pauses or sighs between cues. These choices have little to do with what is really going on in the scene. If you do little or no preparation, the least you should consider when you create a scene is to know "**who**" you are talking to, react to them and to create their presence for the audience. The scene dialogue should not be just a wall-to-wall recitation of lines but instead a well thought out pattern of dialogue, which takes into consideration the intellectual, emotional, physical and spiritual universe of the character. Let's stop here a moment and define these four character attributes.

INTELLECTUAL:

This is what a character intellectually believes within his/her universe. It goes to the core of the things they do. It could be as simple as Democrat or Republican but it can go deeper about their understanding of the world they live in. Characters are often thrust into situations that force them to make decisions based upon logic rather than emotion. This is often the case in business decisions where statistics or numbers are involved or following the forensic evidence to solve a murder mystery. However, an intellectual choice can also be based upon a belief system within the character. Some factor causes them to calculate and then act upon a decision that is centered on facts and data rather than feelings. Think about events in your life where you have responded in an intellectual manner.

EMOTIONAL:

This is what a character feels about themselves and the other characters they relate to in their universe. What is the primary emotion that dominates their existence and how does it effect what they do and what happens to them. Certain situations demand an emotional response. What a characters feels becomes more important than what they think or intellectually rationalize in a given situation. In 1916, there was a shark attack on a little boy in an inland Florida lagoon. It was unbelievable to think that a shark would swim that far inland from the ocean. But it happened. As the shark attacked the seven year old, an adult man jumped into the water and attempted to pull him to safety. The shark killed them both, but there is more to it than that. The underlying motivation for the rescuer was to save the boy despite the intellectual danger and the fear of being torn apart himself. Perhaps it was fear itself that drew the man into the water. In either case, it was a totally emotional response. By the way, this real life event was partially the inspiration for the movie JAWS (1975). Think about moments in your life where you have responded to a stimulus in a purely emotional manner. Maybe it was a time when you someone told you they loved you or learned of someone's death.

PHYSICAL:

How does a character physically interact with the universe they live in? How do they move? How do they interact physically with other characters? Much of our physical response to the world is filtered through our culture and the times we live in. You could be on a subway car in New York City pressed just inches away from another individual standing next to you reading a newspaper. Actually so close to them that you could smell what they ate for breakfast and not think anything of it because the physicality of that universe, space and situation makes it so. You could take the same physical situation and place it on a line at the supermarket in Los Angeles where someone is pressed up against your back as you wait at the check out line and you would perceive that person touching you as invading your space. A character's physical interaction with the universe that surrounds them can also be influenced by culture or time period. What is acceptable in one culture or time period may not be acceptable in another. For example, in western culture, the manner in which opposite sexes touched one another in public during the Victorian era was quite different from the way men and women touch each other today.

SPIRITUAL:

Spirituality goes beyond religious conviction of any particular religion to the core of a character's belief system. Spirituality is a character's moral core and how they perceive what is right and wrong within their universe.

Certain characters find themselves on a journey of discovery and their motivation is centered on that journey. Certainly, Don Quixote's quest in Man of La Mancha would be an example. But a character doesn't have to be on a life long quest to find the meaning of life to have a spiritual motivation. The spirituality of a character can simply be an exploration of an aspect of that character's inner being. This inner being defines privately who they are, what they consider valuable and how they operate within their universe.

How are these elements of intellectual, emotional, physical and spiritual conveyed? How do you do it? The bottom line is to react to the universe around you... point to point with no preconceived notion of what a character will do. This doesn't mean that you are going to change what you have analyzed and rehearsed; it means that you will take each moment as it happens and respond intellectually, emotionally, physically or spiritually to it. When Shakespeare's Macbeth ponders whether or not he should murder Duncan who is his friend and king. He speaks aloud to himself:

First, as I am his kinsman and his subject,

Strong both against the deed; then, as his host,

Who should against his murderer shut the door,

Not bear the knife myself.

Macbeth is rationalizing intellectually that he cannot kill Duncan because he is the king and should be protected within his house. But there is also emotion at play. Macbeth is consumed by the overriding emotion of ambition, which drives him to murder the king despite his intellectual ambitions.

I have no spur

To prick the sides of my intent, but only

Vaulting ambition, which o'erleaps itself

And falls on th' other -

So where can you start to apply these ideas. Start by allowing whom ever your character is speaking to react to what is being conveyed. This is what we do in life. We are put in certain situations with individuals and we react to them. How you react intellectually, emotionally, physically and spiritually around your friends and family members is quite different than how you would react to someone outside that circle – let's say a teacher, doctor, police officer or someone you have just met. A character inhabits the universe of within a scene. They speak the lines and then allow the other characters and the audience to respond. I'm not talking about long dramatic pauses. Just give them a beat to receive and respond to your lines or actions. Even if they don't respond audibly, you need to give them time to react. If you do this, your presentation will be more than a mere recitation of the words of the script in which you race through the lines before you forget them. Allow the other character to absorb what you are saying and doing. Just to jump cue to cue. In addition, don't forget to respond to other characters within the space you have created. Look at them, react to them and allow them to react to what your character is doing within the piece.

What's The Best Way To Memorize My Lines And Create A Physical Life For My Character?

I have heard many actors complain: *"I knew the lines outside in my car or in my house but now, on the stage, I just can't remember anything."* When I hear this type of statement, I know what they have forgotten to do is create a physical life for their character. They fall into the trap of thinking about their scene as just a recitation of lines rather than a slice of a character's life. This means that the moment that we experience a character speaking, it is part of a much larger mosaic. A play or film script contain three components which are available to an actor when performing a scene. They are DESCRIPTION, ACTION and DIALOGUE. What a lot of actors concentrate on is dialogue. They try to memorize lines as a speech and do nothing else. When they stand up on stage or in front of a camera, they try to remember this isolated dialogue and suddenly everything goes blank. Why, they have forgotten to include description and action. To make mattes worse, they learn the dialogue within a physicality that has nothing to do with the reality of the scene they will perform. They work on lines while driving in their car (sometimes on the way to class), watching television or lying down on a couch. Then when they get on their feet for the first time, their brain cannot connect to the new physicality. When preparing to perform a scene don't forget the description of your character and the setting. Also pay attention to what is written about the physical life of the character. What I mean is the physical connection to where the character is and what they are doing as they speak. Creating a physical life will go a long way in helping you to memorize the lines. Your ability to memorize what your character is saying will be connected to a specific physical reality and idea. Your brain will connect what is being said to a specific movement and place. However, you cannot move without purpose. What kind of universe does the character live in and how do they move within it? A character's universe has everything to do with the actual space from which they speak, the time period they live in and **who** they are speaking with. All of this preparation is best done before you perform on a stage in front of an audience or in front of a camera. Try as best as you can to rehearse with your scene partner. We will talk more later about selecting a scene partner.

Creating An Implementation Strategy That Works

WHAT IS AN IMPLEMENTATION STRATEGY?

Think of an implementation strategy as a plan to create a frame or foundation to build and present a scene. The implementation strategy becomes the concept for presentation. Whatever the purpose of your preparation for presentation should include an implementation strategy. You may think it is the director's job to create the framework of the character's physicality and emotion and that you should not have to concern yourself with the details of how it will be presented. The truth is the "*who*" and the "*how*" are indelibly connected. It is like the chef who labors over the preparation and ingredients making up a particular dish, forgetting presentation and just throwing his creation onto a paper plate. In that very act, the chef negates the creative process that taken place before. An actor is no different; consideration of presentation is just as important as character preparation. While an actor cannot control all aspects of presentation, the development of an implementation strategy will create a foundation for the actor to rely upon.

Creating A Performance Dynamic – How To Make A Creative Box To Play In

The dynamic of any presentation takes into consideration all of the physical characteristics of the performance space, the performer's relationship to that space, the distance of the intended audience to the performer, the composition of the intended audience, the surrounding reality of the performance and ultimately the purpose of the performance itself. The dynamics of any given performance can change as the physical characteristics of the space change. While it is virtually impossible for any performer to know totally the dynamic of every audition performance in advance, it is possible to develop a strategy of presentation, based upon what elements are available.

For an acting class, you should be somewhat familiar with the dynamics of the studio space and the distance your audience will be from the performance. Also, find out where the light is within that space. Is it general lighting or like many acting studios do several fixed spotlights light the space? Try to find the light and create your action within that space. On many occasions, students will bring in scenes for performance in my acting classes and set them at the darkest portion of the stage. I often have to reset the scene before they begin so that it is in the light and can be seen by the rest of the class.

For an audition, you can only assume the dynamics of the space and distance to the intended audience. You might be required to present a scene in an office setting, a conference room, or an empty stage. The best strategy is to develop a plan for all three and be prepared for any variation you might encounter. In an audition dynamic, the person you are auditioning for may be looking for a specific element and not your total performance. They also may be multi tasking (making notations, conferring with an associate or looking at your resume) while you are in the midst of the performance. Lastly, the reality you attempt to create might be interrupted by an outside source such as a telephone, people entering the space or the casting person themselves.

The **Presentation Dynamic** is literally the creative box you get to play in. It is the creative framework, which is made up of your character's world, and the actual physical elements within a specific performance environment all rolled into one. It could be a stage space, an outdoor location, a camera angle, or a casting office that your character must evolve within. Caution, when presenting a scene for an acting class or an audition try not to over embellish the space to create a presentation dynamic. If a scene takes place in a restaurant, set a table, chairs, utensils etc.... but don't create the entire restaurant. Just focus on clearly delineating the space so that it is clearly defined for an audience. Once you have established this creative framework, there is a multitude of possibilities that are present within that dynamic at that particular moment in time.

Using "What If?"

You have made the choices detailing **who, what, where and when**. Now, let your character ask him/herself the question: "***What If?***" one of these choices weren't so? Example: You are Romeo quietly watching Juliet standing on her balcony.

Who: A Montague (who falls in and out love) and enemy of the Capulet's

What: Spying upon Juliet as she speaks her private thoughts

Where: The Capulet's orchard, Verona - a place he should not be.

When: Nighttime after the Capulet feast.

Romeo sees the love of his life but cannot muster the will to speak. As she speaks each line, he falls deeper and deeper into silence. He succumbs to his fear and gets up to run away when at the last possible moment, despite his fear, he hears Juliet say:

Romeo, doff thy name,

And for that name which is no part of thee

Take all myself!

When Romeo hears this, his fear vanishes in an instant and he speaks! Why? He knows he can get it all.

I take thee at thy word:

Call me but love, and I'll be new baptized;

Henceforth I never will be Romeo

Using the "**What if?**" you are choosing to play the moment as if this time it will be different. You are playing this scene and speech as if he were going to walk away and somehow this play, at this moment in time is different than any other that has happened before. The key to playing the "*what if?*" is that a character must believe it and more importantly the audience must believe that the "*what if?*" is going to change the outcome. Fight the logical inclination to say to yourself, **this is Shakespeare or this is the text, it cannot be changed**. I am not suggesting a change in text, only a change in intention. We often play the end of the scene because there is a preconceived notion by both performers and audiences as to how it all turns out. We need to recreate that notion in the form of "*what if?*" Let the audience sit on the edge of their seats and wonder if that maybe just this time, at this moment, Romeo just might walk away. What would happen then? Using this approach makes your work unpredictable and interesting.

Creating The "Moment Before."

Where have you come from and what has just happened the moment before?

Within the reality of your character, what moment has the character just left before they entered the moment the scene begins? What was significant about that moment and how will that moment before influence the intellectual, emotional, physical and spiritual state of your character as the scene unfolds? Within this creative framework, the actor then can convey the thoughts of the character, as they would appear in the full presentation of the work. Playing the moment before the lights go up or the camera rolls then allows the audience to catch a character in the midst of their existence living their life in its entirety. The moment before propels a character into "NOW."

Creating "Now" Using Objectives And Beats

WHAT IS YOUR CHARACTER'S MAIN OBJECTIVE?

By speaking the lines in the scene and living the moment, what does your character desire to have happen when the scene is over? Ask yourself, **why** is my character saying and doing this now? What is your character's desired outcome?

WHAT ARE YOUR CHARACTER'S SUB-OBJECTIVES? MARK THEM AS INDIVIDUAL BEATS.

Are there smaller objectives or beats a character must overcome in order to achieve their main objective? A beat could be a small section of the dialogue or movement within the scene. Create a series of beats within the scene to identify sub-objectives. For example, what would Romeo's sub-objectives be?

Beat #1   Romeo sees the love of his life at her balcony but cannot muster the will to speak.

Beat #2   She says his name from her balcony, he succumbs to his fear and gets up to run away.

Beat #3   At the last possible moment, despite his fear, he stops when he hears Juliet say:

Romeo, doff thy name,

And for that name which is no part of thee

Take all myself!

Beat #5   When Romeo hears this, his fear, vanishes in an instant.

Beat #6   He speaks.

I take thee at thy word:

Call me but love, and I'll be new baptized;

Henceforth I never will be Romeo

What are the obstacles in the way of achieving your objectives?

In the course of events leading up to, during and after the completion of the scene, can you identify any obstacles, which are preventing your character from achieving his/her desired goals? Are these obstacles generated externally (literally physical elements) or internal (obstacles created from within your character) which prevent them from their objective? Identify these obstacles and create ways to acknowledge and overcome them.

WHAT IS GOING ON NOW ON AT THIS MOMENT?

At the very moment the scene begins, what is actually happening? If you took a snapshot of this moment, what would be its title? If a character comes home holding a bouquet of flowers, kiss his wife and gives the flowers to her, and then telling her that he has lost his job, what is the title you would place under this moment? It can be called many things, perhaps **"losing a job"** or **"loss"** but it would not be called "**Giving her the bouquet**" because that action is not what is really going on. It is just an action, which is part of the overall moment. Have a clear-cut idea of what is really going on in your character's universe at the moment the scene begins.

WHEN IS THIS MOMENT IN TIME?

Once you have established what the true moment is, then address the question is "**when**" is it? Using the example described above, the moment can be described as morning, day or night but more helpful would be the moment after I lost my job or late at night after I have been walking for hours, because I didn't know how I would tell you. It is literally a definition of **"now."** Once you understand this, you will know what to play. But also understand that **"now"** is constantly changing as the moment evolves.

WHERE ARE YOU? WHAT IS THE SPACE YOUR CHARACTER LIVES IN?

Even though you may perform a scene in any number of nondescript spaces, make a decision for your character about specifically where this moment is taking place. Is it a familiar place like at home that you control or public space that you do not control such as on a bus, in an elevator or on a podium in front of a thousand spectators? What is the space? Is it small and confined, larger than life or somewhere in between? Do not confuse this with the Dynamic of Performance (that is more concerned with the physical properties of the performance space) the **"where are you?"** question addresses solely the reality of the character's universe rather than the performance space. Make specific decisions about the space your character occupies when they begin to move and speak.

Creating The "Moment After."

WHERE ARE YOU GOING?

If your character is in a particular space in a particular moment, where will they go next? Is it somewhere specific? Create a concept of motion. Let the words in the scene and the physical life you have in the moments you create propel you to the next.

EVERYONE LIKES TO KNOW WHERE THEY HAVE BEEN AND WHERE THEY ARE GOING

    I am not asking you to predict the future. However, your character and the audience, in a larger sense, should have some idea about where they are going intellectually, emotionally physically and spiritually as a result of the scene-taking place. Everybody loves to peer into the future and know, if even briefly, what the next moment will bring. Even if you don't really have a clear-cut idea of all of it, give your character and the audience a taste of what may come next. An audience, will say, **"Okay, I have watched and listened to this scene. Now, as a result of this scene what's going to happen?"** Answer the question: **"Now that this scene has taken place, this is what's going to happen next."** You have to share with the audience your character's vision of what the next step will be as you take them along with you on that journey.

"What has happened during this journey? (your scene)" After all that has been said and done, has your character changed? Has your character revealed something about themselves or another character? It may be a minute change, but it is a change nonetheless. What happens next? You as the performer and your character have to answer the question: How has the universe changed and because of what occurred in the scene and what will happen next? You do not have to write new lines to the scene but there has to be a sense that something will follow.

HOW DO YOU PLAY THE MOMENT AFTER?

We have come full circle. Your character must have some resolve intellectually, emotionally, physically and spiritually that connects to what is going on within their universe.

HOW DO YOU SHOW THE MOMENT AFTER?

The way your character contemplates on what has just occurred in the scene or how they react emotionally, or how they physically accommodate those changes. The scene does not end when one of the characters utters the last line. It ends when the audience experiences the character's reaction to the last line. The audience wants a sense of the significance of what has transpired and glimpse of what will be. That is what keeps them invested in your character, they want to know and be part of what is going to happen next. The scene, even though it is a sample, should propel the audience forward and make them want to know what's going to happen next.

At the end of the classic film CASABLANCA (1943) the final lines of the film end this part of the story but also propel the audience into the future when Rick and Captain Renault walk off into the fog to join the Free French Army: " ***"Louis, I think this is the beginning of a beautiful friendship."*** While the audience doesn't know everything that will happen, they do know that because of what has taken place that the world for these two characters will be different than it has been before.

How Do I Begin A Scene At An Acting Class Or Audition?

You have done your preparation, now its time to present? For an acting class, you should be familiar with the space and hopefully rehearsed in it several times. When you are called, you and your partner should quietly set up whatever elements, set pieces, or props you will need. If you are using any type of recorded music or sound effects, I strongly suggest doing a sound check in advance to make sure the levels will work. You may be thinking, use of music or sound? Isn't that a bit over the top for a scene in an acting class? Not really, just as long as it's not a seven piece band. Sometimes a script may have a specific cue for music and the characters comment on the song within the scene. I've also had actors use recorded sound for background. I remember a scene brought to class from the play INHERIT THE WIND by Robert Edwin Lee and Jerome Lawrence where the two main characters were sitting on a porch on a summer night. The actors chose to have the recorded sound of crickets playing on an IPhone in the background that made the scene seem very authentic. It was a simple sound cue that went a long way to create a reality of the scene. Once you are ready to go, cue the teacher and begin. It's so important that you do not speak during the set up about the scene. Things like how few rehearsals you had, that it was difficult to find time to work with your partner or that you have been very busy at work. This is your time to perform not to explain or complain. You may choose to do an introduction to the scene in which you might want to say something about the play or film, who the characters are and perhaps in what part of the story the scene takes place within the whole body of the work. You can also do a similar button at the end of the scene. In either case, when you are ready to begin, cue your acting teacher and start the scene. Once you begin, remember a scene does not have to begin with a line of dialogue. It can begin with an action. When you do this, remember what we discussed about the moment before. Let the scene's beginning be a reaction to whatever occurred the moment before. Now let's talk about start a scene for an audition.

If you have been asked to do a prepared scene as an audition, it will most likely be for a theatrical agent (theatre, TV and film) considering you for representation. If you have gotten his far, it means they like the way you look (your type) and now want to see what you can do with prepared material. You may have already given them your reel which has all sorts of scenes in it but yet they want you to come in and do one live. They want to see you live not through an edited filter and want to see a scene rather than a monologue for several reasons. First, most theatrical agents feel monologues are more appropriate for the stage and secondly they want to see how you react as well as how you deliver lines. Most of the time, these types of scenes are done in the agent's office or conference room so intimacy is often a consideration. When you enter the audition space, get a sense of the room. What is the energy level of the people inside? Where are they sitting? In front of you, on the side or both? How large is the space? What is the distance between where you will perform and the people watching you? What is the acoustic quality of the space? Where is the light and are there any seats or other set materials in the space? Adjust to any deficiencies on the fly. If it is a larger space like a conference room or even a stage and there is an object in your way from a previous audition, it is okay to use it or move it out of the way. Try to make the space as accommodating for your performance as you can. Make the space your own as you create the universe of your character.

If you are required to talk to them before you perform or do a verbal set up which might include the scene title and a little bit of background about the source material and setting, try to be as concise as possible. Try not to use words like **"um" or "like"** and don't comment of extraneous things like how heavy traffic was, that there was no parking or how late you worked the night before. Instead, be very specific and state the name of the source material and a short summary of the portion of the source material that you are performing and what (if anything) is unique about it. You can prepare this in advance and memorize as part of the overall presentation. If the situation calls for you to go right into the scene take some time to create the universe that your character lives in. If there is a bit of conversation before you perform make sure you allow adequate time to separate the reality of the **"audition conversation"** and the reality of the **"universe of the character"** you are to perform. Don't be a **good soldier** and go instantaneously from an interview into a character. You will not totally achieve the transition and your performance will seem uneven and full of distractions. Before you speak, take a moment to let your character's universe surround you. However, please don't do warm ups, stretch out or lower your head toward the floor as you **get into character** then suddenly face forward as the character in a totally different physicality. This caveat may seem elementary but I see actors do it all the time.

Remember, what we discussed earlier, that a prepared scene does not begin with the first line spoken. It begins with the moment before the first line, which causes a character to say the first line or do a physical action. A scene can begin with a physical action or creation of an emotional or physical state by the character. If you are playing Romeo, ask yourself what causes this character say:

"My lips, two blushing pilgrims, ready stand

To smooth that rough touch with a tender kiss."

The answer is that he see's Juliet and immediately falls in love with her. He just doesn't speak those words because Shakespeare wrote them. There is an underlying moment that occurs before the lines are spoken that drives the character to speak those words. When your character speaks those first words in the scene, let them be a reaction to a previous intellectual, emotional or physical moment. This can be a previous moment in the play, film, or something the audience has not even seen. It is a moment that exists in the life and universe of the character. How you play this reaction to a previous moment has all to do with your character's intellectual, emotional, physical and spiritual connection. Ask yourself the question, what does my character **"think"** about this situation, how does my character **"feel"** right now and how does my character respond **"physically"** to this place and situation. And what are your character's beliefs about the nature of their universe and what is right and what is wrong? Once you have answers to these questions, you will have something to play.

Where Should I Look When I Perform A Scene For An Acting Class Or Audition?

This may seem like a silly question to pose in this book. However, it has been my experience both in acting class and when I was an auditioner that actors would constantly break the reality of their scene to look directly at me. The reason for this may be that they want some sort of connection to the acting teacher or auditioner or they may simply want to see how they are doing. In either case, this is not a good choice to make for several reasons. You shatter the reality you are trying to create for your character and more importantly you are putting the acting teacher or auditioner in the awkward position of having to acknowledge you instead of making notes on your scene. If you are thinking about doing a scene, which is presentational, where you interact with and acknowledge the audience looking at them might be okay. However, I don't recommend a presentational type scene for an audition. Casting directors or agents for the most part don't want to be part of your scene. You are there for an audition and this means you must allow them the space to watch and make notes during your performance. If you do acknowledge the audience, select a certain persons or areas of the space to address rather than talking literally over their heads to some random spot. Some acting teachers direct their students to speak **just above the heads** of their audience. I don't like this practice because it is distracting to watch and does not allow the person performing the most effective method of connecting the audience to your character. I think a better choice would be to interact with the other character in the scene as if the audience is not present. Make the universe of your character separate from that of the acting class or audition. Ultimately, I am not one for rules, if you perform a scene and acknowledge the auditioner, you will not fall through a hole in the floor. You can do anything you want to do to create the best reality for your specific scene.

How Do I End My Scene At An Acting Class Or Audition?

In a typical production setting, when a scene in a play is over the lights might fade and come up on another part of the stage or another character might speak in a different area of the stage. In a film, another character can speak; they could cut to the next scene or fade to black. In an acting class or audition setting, you will not have the same control over the space in which you will perform. You will not be able to end the scene with a slow fade of the lights or as in film cut to the next shot. In addition, there may be harsh lighting; exterior noise or it may not be a performance space at all. I have seen several methods of ending a prepared scene for an acting class or audition that I suggest that **you not do.** The first, at the end of the scene, the actors just bow their head toward the floor as if to say, **"its over – you can applaud now."** As you can imagine this unnatural ending is abrupt and solicits what may be an artificial applause and response from the audience. Natural unsolicited applause belongs in a live theatrical performance. You may actually experience natural unsolicited applause in an acting class and that is fine as long as it is not solicited. The second method that you should not do is at the end of the scene when one or more of the actors say the word **"scene."** This is a verbal cue spoken out loud to the acting class or auditioner indicating that the scene is over. This method is also unnatural and creates an abrupt almost jarring ending. I've seen one actor in a scene exit and another remain on stage taking a moment when off stage the voice of the other actor is heard saying **"scene"** giving the scene a very unnatural ending. In addition, actors who use this method of scene ending have a tendency to physically comment upon their work when they say **"scene."** They complete scene and then in a very different physicality look up at the acting teacher or auditioner shrug their shoulders upward in apology and say **"scene."** This is not an ending; it is an apology. It is as if the actor says to the acting teacher or auditioner, ***"I'm so sorry for making you sit through this awful scene."*** All of these artificial methods don't allow the scene to end naturally. What then, should you do?

If we operate on the assumption that you are not directly addressing your acting teacher or auditioner during the scene, then ending your scene is very simple. You complete the last line or action of the scene and then allow a moment after to occur. This allows both the audience and your scene partner to react to that last moment. You take this short beat, then change your physicality from the characters in the scene **back** to your own or neutral position and look directly at and acknowledge the acting teacher or auditioner. This will tell them that the reality you both created for the scene has now ended and that you are back at the in the class or audition. You don't solicit applause or any reaction for that matter. If the audience in the acting class or auditioner want to applaud, they can but it will be a natural reaction to what you have created.

All you are communicating to the acting teacher or auditioner is that the scene is now over. Let them decide how they want to react. The acting teacher may at that point ask you questions and give you notes on your performance. They may even request that you repeat certain portions to illustrate a choice. The auditioner normally will say **"thank you"** and that is it. They may comment on your performance, give specific notes or ask you additional questions about your availability or credits on your resume. Remember; don't comment on your performance in the scene because it is a losing proposition either way. If you say, **"Wow, that was terrible. I can't believe how bad that was."** They may not have felt that way. Alternatively, if you say, **"Wow, was that hot or what? I can't believe how well we just nailed it today."** In this case, they may also not agree. Best bet is to not comment at all and let them do the talking. If an auditioner asks that you perform portions again and provides notes, listen to them carefully and try to incorporate them into a second performance. Many times an auditioner will give notes just to see how you take direction and incorporate their comments into your performance. If you don't understand what they want, don't be afraid to ask and clarify.

How Do I Select A Scene Partner For An Acting Class Assignment Or Audition?

This might be a touchy subject for some of you but remember what I said earlier that all actors should also be producers. The person whom you choose to work with within a scene should be thought about very carefully for both an acting class and an audition. This means you have to think like a producer and pick the appropriate person to work with:

CHARACTER TYPE

You want to select someone who is the right character "type" for the characters in the scene. What is character type? For your scene this has to do with the appropriate age range, physicality and demeanor (energy/outward energy) for the character in the play or film scene. If you have a limited group of students within an acting class try to pick material that generally fit both of your age ranges. One of my pet peeves in many acting scene books that are used in colleges is they have many of the classic plays like Chekov, Ibsen, Brecht or O'Neil where the characters for the most part are often older than the 18-23 demographic for college students. This forces the students to play characters older than they really are and more importantly characters they will never play professionally for decades. I am not saying that actors should not learn the classics but it becomes an exercise in futility to have a twenty year old play a sixty-year old man. Yes, with talcum powder and wigs we can do it but it really serves no learning purpose for the actor. So, try to select a scene that generally fits your age range and if you can your physicality and demeanor.

In an audition, the casting of a prepared scene is just as important as an acting class with one other addition to character type. If you are doing a prepared scene as an audition for a talent agent, you will want to pick a scene partner that is a different acting type than you are. I cannot tell you how many time actors have asked their friends to do a scene with them for an agent and the friend who is the same gender and casting type gets the agent instead of the actor who had the appointment. I recommend trying to pick mixed gender or mixed age range scenes so that both actors have the opportunity to be considered and they are not competing with each other for the same client spot in the agency.

TALENT, SKILLS AND COMMITMENT

Most acting classes have class members that are the stars within the micro universe of acting students. They are the sought after people that everyone wants to do scenes with because of their look, their talent or the success of their previous scene work in the class. In an acting class, of course you want to select someone to work with that has a demonstrated track record of success. This type of person will do the required work, show up to rehearse and be a true partner in getting the scene up on its feet. You don't want to have a scene partner that has a poor reputation in the class, one who isn't available to rehearse. You must also take into consideration their commitment to the class. Some students take an acting class and literally take up space. They do very little work in the class and generally do not contribute to the growth of their fellow classmates. Stay away from these type of people because they will bring you down to their level instead of you bringing them up to your level. If you have any doubts about a person you have selected, talk to them. If they are not available to talk or don't answer your communications discuss what is happening with your acting teacher and make a change.

This becomes paramount in an audition setting. If you are doing a prepared scene for an audition, you want someone who is prepared to put the work in that needs to be to achieve a positive result.

A reason **"not"** to pick someone to work in a scene with you.

DATING?

You select someone you want to go out with. This may seem crazy but in more than a few of my classes, people love to hang out and pick people to work with that they think they want to go out with. It rarely works because these people rarely want to do any of the work needed to do the scene and are usually dropped from the scene and many times the class.

How Do I Rehearse A Scene For An Acting Class Or Audition?

1. Meet with your partner and select a scene and set up a specific rehearsal schedule up and including the due date. Exchange contact information.
2. Read through it for content and make cuts if needed
3. Come up with a collective point of view to present the scene.
4. Each person should make a list of props, costume and set requirements - you can do this by setting up column space on each side of the script and making notations as you read through it.
5. Get it on its feet - either block in advance or sketch out a rough blocking set and let your character move through it. Once a pattern is established, you can set it. Also make note of any "physical business" such as fights, dance type sequences - these must be set in advance.
6. Set specific goals for your character - Make sure you know the following:
   What does my character want in the total scene?
   > Break the scene down into beats and set sub goals for each beat which lead toward the total scene goal.

   Where has my character come from just before the scene?
   Where is my character going or what has changed as a result of the scene.
   Lastly, think about -

Intellectual - What does my character think about this situation?

Emotional - How does my character feel about this situation?

Physical - How does my character move and experience the space in relationship to other characters or objects in the space?

Spiritual – What are my character's beliefs and values?

Work together and come to a consensus on how the scene will be presented.

What If The Script Is Too Long Or Too Short?

Read entire piece out loud with feeling. Time the length of the reading. Subtract the allotted time the piece should be from your timed reading. Do not be afraid to "cut" all the extraneous material--even if you like it--the audience will not know it was there. Decide on the main thought or theme that goes through the scene. Remember that the purpose of the scene is to show your character. Cut all extraneous material that does not fit into what you have decided for your character and the scene as a whole. Give the lines of one character to another and cut the character if the character is unnecessary to the plot line. Read piece aloud at the end of the cutting session to time it. Follow this procedure until the "cutting fits the allotted time."

Also, when doing a film script you may have to combine several portions of a single scene together that have be separated by time or location. You many have two characters at one location talking, then the script may cut away to something that is happening elsewhere and then cut back. Scenes can also be cut because of flashbacks or time cuts. Don't be afraid to edit the appropriate pieces together to give the scene a more complete feel. Caution, when doing a film scene, don't feel you are obligated to do exactly what is in the film. Remember, you are now acting in the scene and choices should be centered on what you and your partner are trying to achieve rather than what might be contained in a film that has already been shot.

Presenting - In Class Versus For An Audition

CREATING A POINT OF VIEW:

In a performance setting you will have a director to guide you through the process. A good director will normally state a point of view for the film or play. That is state the manner and direction in which they intend to present the material. For example: Romeo and Juliet was presented in a traditional manner with costume and setting of the period implied by Shakespeare by Franco Zeffirelli in 1968 or modernized as in the version directed by Baz Luhrmann in 1996. The Point of View is how the director chooses to present the material. In a class presentation, scene partners must derive a point of view for their presentation and experiment around that agreed upon idea. The point of view should be established before the actual rehearsals begin so that both actors are focused upon one presentational goal.

EXPERIMENTATION DURING REHEARSAL – TRY NEW THINGS BUT THEN MAKE SPECIFIC CHOICES

During experimentation, you will discover that not all choices work. Keep the choices that work for you and discard what does not work. Remember
You cannot play all things in one performance.

Play your character moment to moment.
Be a reactor. Listen and feel and respond accordingly. Experimentation is part of the creative process. However, at some point specific choices must be made and then incorporated into the final presentation.

Creating An Interesting Character

What should you consider when creating a scene either with a scene partner or as part of a professional performance?

CREATING A CHARACTER

After reading the play or screenplay several times make the following notes about your character. If you read the entire script (and you should) how are the three "P's" answered about your character?

Personal: Are they married, single divorced? Live alone?

Professional: What do they do? Are they a doctor, lawyer, spy?

Private: Some secret about your character that only they know. For example, a war hero who is really (privately) a coward.

READING THE SCRIPT

What does the writer say about my character?

How does the writer describe your character when they are first introduced to the audience?

What does my character do that is revealing about their personality?

How do they enter the space when first introduced?

What does my character say about themselves?

Does your character ever speak about themselves in the form of description or telling of some experience?

What does my character do?

What are your character's actions within the universe of the play or film?

What do other characters say about your character?

How do other characters in the story describe your character? Do their descriptions agree or disagree with your own character's description of themselves.

How do other characters react when your character enters the space?

Do they react in a certain way or not react at all?

Setting Objectives For Your Character

MACRO: CREATE AN OBJECTIVE FOR THE ENTIRE PIECE.

Look at the entire play or screenplay and create a super **objective** for your character within the entire piece. This can be stated in terms of "My character wants... by the end of this play or movie." This could be a simple phrase: *My character wants to be a real boy* – Pinocchio or *My character wants to get his boat back* - Jack Sparrow in Pirates of the Caribbean

MICRO: CREATE OBJECTIVES FOR EACH SCENE

Make a list of each scene your character appears.

How does that scene fit into the overall macro objective?

What is your character's objective within each scene?

What are the barriers in that scene, which have to be overcome in order to meet that objective?

*Note: In Live Theater you may hear the term **FRENCH SCENE** - this is a term that refers to your character's objectives or central purpose between each entrance and exit.

OBSTACLES

What is preventing your character from achieving what they want? Within a scene, creating smaller divisions within the body of a scene. Each beat or unit should be tied to a particular physicality or piece of business. You may create smaller objectives or obstacles within each beat or unit. Once you have created the list consider the following questions:

1) Who will be in the scene? Which characters? The point of view character needs to present.
2) Where is it taking place? In a living room, a restaurant, in a car?
3) When? What is the time of day, season, year, etc.?
4) What is happening? Is there a problem? Are they just talking? Drinking coffee or a beer? Is someone pacing?
5) Why are they there? Invited to dinner, barged in or sneaked in through the servants entrance and are eavesdropping?
6) What are the motives of the other characters and how are they involved in your character's objectives. Are they supportive or do these serve as an obstacle? Are they suspects, victims, or witnesses?
7) What has just happened the moment before and what is about to happen?

For each question you can use the five senses to take notice of all the little things that will be the windows in which your character senses the world around them.

A word about PRIMARY and SECONDARY characters in a scene. A primary character is the one the scene is about. A secondary character simply serves the character or plot line. These types of supernumerary characters are messengers, waiters or characters with a single line. If you are the pizza delivery boy and you have one scene in which you deliver a pizza. Just deliver the pizza. That is your objective within the story.

CREATE AN OBJECTIVE FROM YOUR OWN INTERPRETATION

This is just a random sampling of sample objectives. You can look up additional ones in a dictionary or thesaurus.

To ABANDON	To BADGER	To DARE
To ABASE	To BAIT	To DEFY
To ABASH	To BEFRIEND	To DEGRADE
To ABET	To BEG	To DEMEAN
To ABHOR	To BELITTLE	To DEMORALIZE
To ABDICATE	To BEMUSE	To DENOUNCE
To ALLY	To BERATE	To DEPRECATE
To ABSOLVE	TO BESEECH	To DERIDE
To ABSORB	To BEWILDER	To DISARM
To ABUSE	To BOTHER	To DISGUST
To ACCEPT	To BRIBE	To DISILLUSION
To ACCLAIM	To BULLY	To DISSUADE
To ADMONISH	To CHASTEN	To ELUDE
To ADVISE	To CHASTISE	To EMASCULATE
To AFFRONT	To CHIDE	To EMBARRASS
To AGGRAVATE	To CON	To ENCHANT
TO ALTER	TO COERCE	TO ENCOURAGE

56 Setting Objectives For Your Character

To AMUSE	To COMFORT	To ENLIGHTEN
To ANIMATE	To COMMAND	To ENRAGE
To ANNIHILATE	To CONVINCE	To ENSLAVE
To ANNOY	To CONFER	TO ENTICE
To ANTAGONIZE	To CONFOUND	To ENTREAT
To AROUSE	To CONSOLE	To EXCITE
To ATTACK	To COURT	TO FLATTER

Actions, intentions, goals, or needs, as they are also known--refer to an inner drive, **something your character needs to do to, or wants to get from**, another character. It is essentially what you "act." You create a drive that causes the character to do and say things aimed at getting what they want. Just as in life all our words and behaviors stem from what we want from the people around us, our characters are likewise driven by needs or objectives.

In the course of a play or movie a character's dramatic through-line is made up of behaviors that are propelled by need.

"There is something I want and I take this action,

I observe your response to evaluate if what I am doing and saying is working,

I adjust my actions based on your response,

I try again."

It is a continuous, unbroken thread that, as an actor, you connect to each time you go the play or scene begins. Every moment of the performance, a character should be focused on achieving an objective in one way or another.

How To Have Fun At An Acting Class Or Audition

This last note will sound strange and a bit cliché' but if you are having a good time your acting teacher and auditioner will be more likely to become engaged in the intellectual, emotional, physical and spiritual life of the characters you create. Acting classes by their very nature should be enjoyable experiences. However, many students find the criticism they get in an acting class too personal in nature. Often there is an underlying insecurity in what they do that goes beyond simple criticism of their acting abilities. We all have individuals around us that support us and then we also have the others that tear us down. In my classes, I always couch my criticism with praise by saying something the student has done well and then what they need to work on. I was a guest in an acting class one evening where the acting teacher berated the student's physical appearance and acting ability. That's not my style. So how to make an acting class fun? Answer: Enjoy the journey and don't make it personal. Make it a game that you play and enjoy but one that is separate from what you do when you go home at night. Yes, an acting career is challenging and requires a life long commitment. However, it's only part of your life and who you are. If you get one of those drill sergeant type of acting teachers, drop the class if you find that type of criticism bothersome. On the other side of coin some students want intense negative and personal criticism.

Attending an audition is similar to an acting class because you are also being judged. However, the very nature of an audition is selection for a particular project. It is and should never be personal. Always remember an audition is a presentation for a creative project at a specific moment in time. Once that audition is over, let it go. Have no vested interest in it put it behind you and forget it. If you got the part they will contact you if you didn't, there will be another audition tomorrow. If you are doing a prepared scene for an agent, they are looking at you in relationship to the other clients they already represent. If you fit a space in their client list, you will be selected for representation. If there is a conflict you will not. I always have believed that the universe wants to provide great things to us… but we often hold on the lesser things because we are afraid. My advice for a fun audition? Let go! However it turns out just have a great time doing it and remember why you wanted to be in actor in the first place. If you feel good about what you are doing, you will do it better. Can you visualize that first moment you had the thought that you wanted to be an actor? Maybe you were watching television, a movie or a play. You sat in your seat and you thought to yourself.

> "I can do that! I want to be up there on the screen or on the stage. I want to do it because it's something I enjoy. No it's something that I love. I love to act because it's inside of me and part of who I am. I can't think of doing anything else!"

Okay, so that seems a bit over the top. But didn't you ever feel this way at least a little bit. Well, I want you to go back to that personal moment for you. Go back to it and remember that you wanted to act because you love it and it makes you happy when you do it. Keep that always in your heart and find joy in what you do. Even if you don't get the part or you get it wrong, it doesn't matter because there will always be another day, another audition and another part to play. Whether it's an acting class or an audition have a great time. Be thankful that you have the opportunity to perform and share your talent. This is not really advice, its common sense. But it goes to the core of why we act. We act because we love to act and that passion should be part of everything that we do.

How To Use This Book

Before you move on to the scene section, I would like to discuss the informational section that precedes each scene. Each scene is preceded with the following information:

TITLE: You may use this title or not in your presentation. In addition, many of the scenes in this book are from larger works such as plays or films. In those instances that information will be included under the title.

GENDER A suggestion of appropriate gender for the characters.

AGE RANGE: States the approximate ages of the characters.

CHARACTERS: Names and description of each character.

LOCATION: General location where the scene takes place.

TIME: Time of day or Historical time period in which the scene takes place.

SYNOPSIS: A general description of what takes place within the confines of the scene.

GENRE: Comedy or Drama or both.

PRODUCTION: (OPTIONAL)

For those scenes that are presented specifically for acting classes rather than auditions, there are suggestions for minimal production elements and presentation suggestions to better connect with the audience or to enhance dramatic effect.

Production suggestions might include the use of props, sound, music or costumes.

Presentation suggestions might include character's acknowledging the audience, slates or asides.

These suggestions are included within the body of the scene and maybe used or ignored as is deemed appropriate for the nature of the presentation.

THE SCENES

#1 THE HIT

GENDER:	(Male/Male)
AGE RANGE:	Adult male 30's – 40's
CHARACTERS:	**THE DON** (adult/male) – crime boss in Staten Island, New York
	LOUIE (adult/male) – the Don's left hand man
LOCATION:	The Don's private office
TIME:	The present – Night
SYNOPSIS:	The Don's nightclub has been vandalized by his crosstown gang rival Frankie Bananas. Now a decision must be made about how to respond.
GENRE:	Comedy

(The Don is still half asleep as Louis enters.)

THE DON
Louie... how come you woke me up in the middle of the night? I was right in the middle of a nice dream...

LOUIE
Don, I'm sorry... But Frankie Bananas and his boys just hit the Kit Kat Club about an hour ago... turned the whole joint upside down.

THE DON
Frankie hit Kit Kat Club?

LOUIE
Yeah... they broke the joint to pieces... smashed all the chairs... even ripped the paper towel holder right off the wall in the men's toilet. Now when you take a dump -- ya'got no way to wash your hands afterwards... I mean that's a health risk...

THE DON
That's disgusting...

LOUIE
So, I came right away to tell you and wanna know if you want me to retaliate? Ya'know... Tit for tat... Ba Da Bing. One... two... tree... take Frankie out... then he's dead... D E D.

THE DON
How you gonna do that?

LOUIE
I know exactly where Frankie's gonna be... an hour from now.

THE DON
Where's that?

LOUIE
At Rudy's... havin a peperoni sandwich.

THE DON
Rudy's on Third Avenue?

LOUIE
Na... definitely not Third Avenue... Rudy's in Brooklyn.

GODFATHER
You sure? I never heard of Rudy's in Brooklyn?

LOUIE
Don, I respectfully disagree... they got a Rudy's in Brooklyn. I been there! Right across from Joey's Cookies...

THE DON
No that's can't be right... Sally's Sausage is across from Joey's Cookies...

LOUIE
No more... Sally's Sausage went out...

THE DON
They went out? I can't believe it... I went to reform school with Sally... Remember he had a daughter with the moustache... I think her name was Mary.

LOUIE
Yeah... that's the one. She was a pretty girl... except for the moustache... I could never get past that... I wonder if she ever got married?

THE DON
I don't know...

(Beat)

What were we talking about?

LOUIE
Frankie Bananas... and Rudy's in Brooklyn...

THE DON
Right... you sure you got the right Rudy's?

LOUIE
My snitch said, "Frankie's goin to Rudy's... "

THE DON
But did he specifically say... "Rudy's in Brooklyn?" They also got Rudy's on 125th.

LOUIE
Na... Rudy's on 125th? Up there? Since when?

THE DON
Maybe six months.

LOUIE
So what's so special about the one on 125th?

THE DON
The one on 125th got a bakery... Frankie Bananas is gonna wanna eat a cannoli with coffee after he eats his pepperoni sandwich... He's gonna go there! I'm telling you.

LOUIE
You know I think you're right... the Rudy's in Brooklyn doesn't have a bakery?

THE DON
No bakery? What the hell good is that?

LOUIE
No fricken good... how the hell can you eat without a bakery? It's always nice to have a little something sweet after you eat... with a cup of coffee.

THE DON
Right. That's what I'm tellin ya... The one on 125th street makes fresh cup cakes.

LOUIE
Cupcakes... with sprinkles?

THE DON
Yeah... they melt in your mouth...

LOUIE
Shut up!

THE DON
Louie, you tellin me to shut up? I'll fricken shoot ya!

LOUIE
No... no... I was talking about the cupcakes... I swear... I was just talkin about those fluffy cupcakes with sprinkles on em... that's all.

(Beat, the Don looks at him menacingly then...)

THE DON
Geeze, I wish I had one of them there cup cakes right now.

LOUIE
Yeah, me too... I'm salivatinn here... like a dog thinkin about a friggin bone...

THE DON
Yeah...

LOUIE
Yeah...

(BEAT, they stop and look at each other.)

THE DON
You up for this?

LOUIE
Don, you kiddin me?

THE DON
Get the car.... we're gonna make a hit...

LOUIE
Yeah...

THE DON
A cupcake hit... at Rudy's.

LOUIE
On 125th?

                    THE DON
Does a bear shit in the fricken woods or what?

                    LOUIE
Fagettaabout it!

#2 AMERICA

GENDER:	(Male/Female)
AGE RANGE:	Adult (20's – 30's)
CHARACTERS:	**JACK** (20'S 30's)– the trainer
	JILL (20's – 30's) - the trainee
LOCATION:	Terrorist training camp somewhere in the Midwest United States
TIME:	The present
SYNOPSIS:	A trainer tests the intellectual skills of his trainee.
GENRE:	Drama

(Jill sits quietly with eyes closed until the silence is interrupted when Jack sits on a chair facing her.)

JACK
Okay Jill, let's try again.

JILL
I'm tired.

JACK
... and you should call me Jack. I said... *again.*

(Beat.)

JILL
I pledge allegiance to the flag of the United States of America… and to the republic for which it stands

(Beat, she struggles to remember the words.)

One nation… under something or other…

JACK
Wrong!

JILL
I'm tired of doing this!

JACK
We're not stopping until you get it right.

JILL
I don't think I'll ever get it right…

JACK
If you are to be accepted… you will have to know it.

JILL
No one will ever ask me this?

JACK
You are wrong! That's the first thing they will ask you.

JILL
Nobody in this country cares about these words.

JACK
They must care about something…

JILL
Reality TV shows and football.

(Beat.)

JACK
I'm impressed...

JILL
...at what?

JACK
That you have thought about it so much as to put those thoughts together all by yourself... let's try again.

JILL
I pledge allegiance...

(Stops)

Why you don't think because I am woman that I can put thoughts together?

JACK
I'm only stating what is a fact.

JILL
I just don't want to waste my time learning words that have no meaning to me.

JACK
It is important that you do this so that you fit in...

JILL
I don't want to fit in... I want to leave this horrid country and go back home! I miss my family... and my life there.

JACK
We are at war... and we will never return to our home. Never.

(Beat.)

JILL
I pledge allegiance to the flag of the United States of America and to the republic for which it stands...

JACK
...and?

JILL
I hate you and your stupid war.

JACK
It is not my war...

JILL
When I first saw your picture on the Internet seeking a bride... I disliked you... you were so unattractive... but now that I know you... I hate you.

JACK
You will be punished for these thoughts... purge them from your heart.

JILL
No! I hate the way you look, the way you smell, the way you breathe when you sleep at night and the sound of your voice when you're awake. I hate all of you...

JACK
You know I could beat you for such words?

JILL
You could **try** to beat me... I'd fight back.

JACK
You know you have become very western.

JILL
I would fight you until my last breath...

JACK
This is not appropriate behavior... you would force me to kill you.

(Beat.)

JILL
What if I kill you instead?

(He confidently smiles.)

JACK
I am stronger than you.

JILL
I curse you...

JACK
I thought **you** wanted to kill me?

JILL
The poison inside of your twisted mind will turn you upon yourself. The pain inside you will grow so intense that you will try to cut it out of your body with a knife.

JACK
So full of hate... my dear Jill, You have truly become the infidel.

JILL
Call me by my real name!

JACK
That name for you no longer exists... I am Jack and you are Jill and we live in America. What we were before is over. This is getting tiresome... let's do this one more time and do it correctly... or I will be forced to cut that pretty face of yours...

(Beat)

NOW DO IT! I'm losing my patience.

(Beat, reluctantly.)

JILL
I pledge allegiance to the flag
Of the United States of America

(Tears fill her eyes)

and to the republic for which it stands. One nation... under God... indivisible...

(Crying)

with liberty and justice for all...

JACK

Excellent...

#3 THE FORTUNE TELLER

GENDER: (Male/Female)

AGE RANGE: (Adult 20's – 40's)

CHARACTERS: **ALLEN WOOD** (20'S - 30's) – a reality TV star and producer.

MADAME ALYEKA (30's – 50's) – a fortuneteller and former circus ventriloquist of vague ethnic origin.

LOCATION: Back room of Madame Alyeka's store front "MYSTERY PARLOR."

TIME: The present

SYNOPSIS: A distraught reality TV producer reaches into the netherworld to find his fiancé and gets a bit more than he bargains for.

GENRE: Comedy

(ALYEKA eyes closed and arms extended outward with palms up, sits humming almost inaudibly then stops when WOOD enters and sits.)

ALYEKA
Come in... I am Madame Alyeka... and you are? STOP! Don't tell me... let me guess. I am sensing a "G" You or someone near you with a "G."

WOOD
No... I'm sorry... no G.

ALYEKA
Wait, the spirits are coming in bit louder now... it's an "N..." There is definitely an "N."

WOOD
Sorry, no.

ALYEKA
Now the spirits are even louder... so loud there giving me a migraine... what about a P? You gotta P?

WOOD
No...

ALYEKA
Everybody's got a "P" sooner or later... Okay, I give up... who are you?

WOOD
My name is Allen Wood...

ALYEKA
Allen Wood? Producer and star of the reality show I'M GETTING WOOD?

WOOD
No, it's called BEING WOOD. Just BEING WOOD.

ALYEKA
Right... where's the camera are we on TV now?

WOOD
No, I'm alone... I saw your sign outside and need your help to find Holly.

ALYEKA
Holly your fiancé on the show? Hey, I watch the show every week Last week's episode, she drove off in your convertible with the swami from Tibet. Great episode ending...

WOOD
Wasn't a planned... she really did disappear with the swami... she told me she was in search of spiritual enlightenment... took all my credit cards and Carrera Porsche convertible. Haven't seen her since. That's why I'm here.

ALYEKA
Holly Wood? Was that going her name on the show after you were married?

WOOD
We talked about it... but now she's gone and without Holly Wood there's no show. We shoot the season finale in two days and have to end it with a wedding. I need you to contact the spirit world... to help me find out where she is...

ALYEKA
Mr. Wood, spirit talk is not cheap. Basic Plan is $80 – includes two talking spirit minutes... after that its $25 per additional minute... or the special **Reach Out Plan** with unlimited spirit minutes and one free apparition for $100.

WOOD
I'm in... all I have is this hundred dollar bill... will you take cash?

(She snaps the hundred from him, takes his hand and reads his palm.)

ALYEKA
No worries... I see I see I see...

WOOD
What do you see?

ALYEKA
Right here... a long road a very long road... someone standing with their arms folded frowning and... judging you... there's torment and ridicule.

WOOD
That my mother... let's not go down that road.

ALYEKA
Okay, Let's go another way... forget the palms... you have sweaty hands anyway.
Let's just dial in... okay?

(She closes her eyes)

I now conjure the spirit realm to help Allen Wood... producer and star of MY MORNING WOOD...

WOOD
BEING WOOD.

ALYEKA
BEING WOOD... I call upon you in the spirit realm to find his two timing fiancé... Holly Wood and save his season finale. Come forth now I command you! Let's help this poor schlep out...

(Alyeka twitches and goes into a trance then speaks with a different accent.)

ALYEKA (AS GINGER)
Allen Wood? Allen Wood... I'm looking for Allen Wood...

WOOD
Here I am! Right here!

ALYEKA (AS GINGER)
You look so much younger in person! I love your show I'M PACKING WOOD...

WOOD
BEING WOOD.

ALYEKA (AS GINGER)
Whatever... I am Ginger R... the spirit of TV future.

WOOD
TV Future? Didn't know they had that?

ALYEKA (AS GINGER)
Actually, there's three of us... past, present... and me... we trade off every six months... I've come from the spirit world to warn you.

WOOD
Warn me about what?

ALYEKA (AS GINGER)
Holly Wood... the actress that plays your fiancé on the show... she's leaving you.

WOOD
I already know that. Tell me something I don't know.

ALYEKA (AS GINGER)
Okay... she did you a favor!

WOOD
A favor?

ALYEKA (AS GINGER)
Her favorability ratings with the 18–30 year old demographic are in the toilet... nobody likes her because she dresses and acts like a money-grabbing slut.

WOOD
That can't be... we pitched it at the network and they loved the comeback angle... **Holly, bad girl from the streets of Detroit redeems herself and makes good.**

ALYEKA (AS GINGER)
Forget comeback... it's more like **Holly, bad girl stays bad girl... rips off her TV fiancée and leaves him high and dry for the pool boy.** Is that the way you want to wind up this season?

WOOD
It could work... but we'd have to slap a happy ending on it

ALYEKA (AS GINGER)
"Happy Schmappy..." Allen... you want happy? Drop Holly like a bad habit and get yourself a new girl.

WOOD
You want me to find a new girl and marry her in one episode? We'd have to go commercial free... to fit all that in.

ALYEKA (AS GINGER)
No more than two minutes of screen time… you got writers?

WOOD
Too many…

ALYEKA (AS GINGER)
Have one of them write a new ending. Give Holly a brain embolism while sky diving over Malibu… she jumps out of the plane but her chute never opens… you can shoot it all on "go pro." Just throw a mannequin out of the plane and follow it down until it splashes into the sea. BLACK OUT! Then, when you go to the beach to find her body (which you never do), you meet a voluptuous lifeguard… **that's** who you marry. It'll be like Baywatch…you remember Baywatch? Well it will be like Baywatch meets the Bachelor… the audience will love it!

WOOD
How am I going to find a voluptuous lifeguard in just two days?

ALYEKA
Alyeka's niece Natalia… she's on the swim team at the community college.

WOOD
Natalia? Can she act?

ALYEKA (AS GINGER)
Acting? Who needs acting? She's a knock out! About your age and height, size five junior petite, with long black hair, dark eyes and good teeth… more importantly a nice personality. Your ratings will go through the roof… like **butter** on a bun.

WOOD
Did you say like butter on a bun? Hello? Hello? Ginger?

ALYEKA (AS GINGER)
You're breaking up… I'm in the canyon. Remember dump Holly… she's a blood sucking ratings loser! Get Natalia. She is your true love… gotta go!

(The voice fades away and Alyeka snaps back up.)

ALYEKA
Wow... my ears are ringing... I feel like I was in a canyon.

WOOD
You were... I spoke to Ginger R the spirit of TV future. Who's Natalia?

ALYEKA
My niece?

WOOD
I have to meet her.

ALYEKA
Why do you want to do that?

WOOD
She is my true love... and my season closer. I'm going to marry her.

ALYEKA
Ginger told you to marry my niece Natalie on television?

WOOD
Yes, and that's exactly what I'm going to do. She's going to be a star! Natalie what a beautiful name... you think she'll marry me?

ALYEKA
To be on TV? Are you kidding me... she'll do it. Then her name would be Natalie Wood?

WOOD
Right... that could work...

ALYEKA
Yes, it could.

#4 GODS AND MONSTERS
from the play *The Resting Place*

GENDER:	(Male/Male)
AGE RANGE:	(Adult 20's – 40's)
CHARACTERS:	**JOSEPH FANELLI** (20'S - 30's) – a fast-talking and successful businessman who is wealthy but his life has no meaning.
	FATHER DONOVAN (30's – 50's) - a Catholic Priest from Ireland wearing a black jacket and white collar.
LOCATION:	**SAINT CATHERINE'S OF SIENA – CHURCH**
TIME:	The present – early in the morning.
SYNOPSIS:	A Catholic confession. Joey Fanelli tortured by his past, seeks answers from a priest Father Donovan
GENRE:	Drama

(OPTIONAL SOUND – Gregorian chant as Joey kneels in front of Father Donovan sitting.)

JOEY
Bless me father… my name is Joseph Fanelli… and I have sinned.

DONOVAN
You may sit… my son.

(MUSIC FADES as Joey sits in a chair opposite Donovan.)

JOEY
Father Donovan... I want to be straight with you. I never really believed in God... when I was a kid my mother forced me to go to church every Sunday... I hated it and the whole mass in Latin thing never appealed to me... I never understood anything that the priest said... seems like a lot of bullshit.

DONOVAN
Do you feel the least bit reluctant to use such language in the house of God?

JOEY
I'm supposed to tell the truth... am I right?

DONOVAN
Yes, but aren't you worried that God might punish you?

JOEY
Like strike me with lightening...

DONOVAN
Something like that.

JOEY
I'm not afraid of God.

DONOVAN
I see, so you're not afraid of anything?

JOEY
Well, almost... when I was a kid in Catholic School... there was one nun... Sister Mary Catherine... she beat the crap out of me a few times. Do you know her?

DONOVAN
No... so you were afraid of her but not afraid of God?

JOEY
When she beat me... I knew that God had no control in my universe... it was the monsters that ran the earth. Ya 'know... the ones that come after you in the night.

DONOVAN
Sister Mary Catherine was one of the monsters?

JOEY
What do think? Yeah she was a monster... just like the Wolf Man or Dracula... they ruled the night... and if you rule in the darkness... you rule the world.

DONOVAN
What about the day?

JOEY
That's when they rest... everybody knows that.

DONOVAN
When you were a child... did you fear the monsters?

JOEY
You bet your ass... but I knew how to survive.

DONOVAN
How did you do that?

JOEY
By keeping the monsters happy. You ask a lot of questions.

DONOVAN
I'm sorry; I'm trying to understand.

JOEY
Really? Don't you just sit there and listen... and then tell me to say a few Hail Mary's?

DONOVAN
I hope to do more than that... when I was a young boy in Ireland... I lost my parents at a very young age and was brought up in a convent. You see I had my own version of Sister Mary Catherine...

JOEY
Did she beat you?

DONOVAN
Often... and if I cried she would hit me harder... sometimes until I bled. So I understand you very well. Let's talk about heaven.

JOEY
What about it?

DONOVAN
Did you ever think that you might want to go to heaven someday?

JOEY
To visit? Not really... I figured it was a lot like Miami Beach... overrated.

DONOVAN
Heaven is a place of eternal happiness with no pain... that's how I survived.

JOEY
Father, when I was a kid I didn't give a shit about heaven... I just was trying to get by on Earth... by keeping the monsters happy.

DONOVAN
Did you make Sister Mary Catherine happy?

JOEY
Sometimes.

DONOVAN
How did you do that?

JOEY
Boy, you are getting personal here... just give me a few prayers to say and let me go.

DONOVAN
That I will do... but first... how did you make her happy?

(Beat, he is reluctant to say.)

JOEY
By letting her touch me... okay! You happy now? She said she was going to cut it off... if I didn't let her touch me... so what the hell, it didn't hurt... I let her do it. That's life father... that's life! Keeping the monsters happy! That's how I survived!

DONOVAN
You could have resisted...

JOEY
And bleed like you? What are you fucking idiot? You keep the monsters happy that's how you do it. Besides I was just a kid.

DONOVAN
But you're a man now... there is another way... prayer and forgiveness.

JOEY
What's that? Say ten Hail Mary's and hope that the monsters will go away... words alone never made the monsters go away.

DONOVAN
There's more... you vanquish them.

JOEY
What?

DONOVAN
In the name of the Lord you cut **them** until **they** bleed and then bury them... in pieces.

JOEY
How would you go about doing that? Like sticking a stake in a vampire's heart?

DONOVAN
Lull them... propitiate upon them... so you can get close and then make them bleed.

JOEY
Wait, are you telling me to kill Sister Mary Catherine... In your book... isn't that a sin?

DONOVAN
Retribution of the righteous is never a sin...

JOEY
You're getting kinda dark on me Father.... wouldn't I go to hell for something like that?

DONOVAN
The Lord never turns away one of his flock.

JOEY
Father, I'm not a sheep... I'm one of the wolves.

DONOVAN
A wolf in trouble... Say ten Our Father's... then go find Sister Mary Catherine... and vanquish the beast...it is the only way you will find peace. Bless you... in the name of the father, the son and the Holy Ghost.

(Father Donovan rises and exists. Joey remains.)

JOEY
How the hell am I going to find her? She must be at least eighty years old by now....

DONOVAN (OFF)

Just do it!

JOEY
Okay... Okay... I'll do it. But first the Our Father's... right?

(Joey kneels again.)

Our Father who art in heaven,

hallowed be thy name.

Thy kingdom come.

Thy will be done on earth, as it is in heaven.

    (OPTIONAL SOUND – GREGORIAN CHANT PLAYS THEN FADES.)

#5 LOOKING
Adapted from the play *Myths and Tangos*

GENDER:	(Male/Female)
AGE RANGE:	(Adult 20's – 40's)
CHARACTERS:	**SETH BAKER** (20'S – 30's) – a man who is many things… in this scene he is a painter.
	DONNA (30's – 50's) - just Donna, no last name. A lonely housewife who wants more out of life than cooking, cleaning and waiting at night until her husband gets home from the office.
LOCATION:	A park bench in a serene setting.
TIME:	The present – late morning.
SYNOPSIS:	Two lonely people have a chance meeting at a park bench and perhaps the start of something much more.
GENRE:	Drama

(Donna turns toward the audience as she sits quietly on a park bench enjoying the fresh air and morning sun.)

DONNA
When a male black tipped hand fly catches a really tasty morsel—maybe a delicious spider or a tender aphid tartar, he may offer it up to a passing female. Like all males, his motive is transparent—he hopes she'll mate with him after he wines and dines her.

(She returns to scene as Seth enters, stops and looks at her.)

SETH

Is it true what they say?

DONNA

Excuse me?

SETH

About taking the time to smell the roses.

DONNA

Yes, right.

SETH

What a great morning to be in the park.

DONNA

Almost like an impressionistic painting… I love the way the sun illuminates the trees.

SETH

A pointillist fantasy.

DONNA

Right…

(To audience)

Is this guy trying to hit on me? Men are likes apes in the jungle.

SETH

I'm Seth Baker… and your name is?

DONNA

Donna… just Donna.

(Seth extends his hand.)

SETH
Please to meet you Donna.

DONNA
Likewise... so, Seth what do you do?

SETH
I'm a painter...

DONNA
Houses?

SETH
No... pictures.

DONNA
A painter painter... how creative.

SETH
Sometimes.

DONNA
I can remember a time when I loved doing creative things more than life itself... I had so much more passion then.

SETH
Passion is very hard to have... what happened?

DONNA
Life... and being preoccupied with making money... success and all that.

SETH
Right... **"Show me the money!"** That's a line from the movie Jerry Maguire... do you remember it... with Tom Cruise?

DONNA
I think so... it's from a long time ago... right?

SETH
Yes... your cheekbones are so compelling... like Botticelli's **Venus.**

(He examines her face.)

DONNA
Venus? I've never been told I look like Venus… thank you.

SETH
The Roman goddess of love.

DONNA
Really?

SETH
I have an art show coming up in a few weeks… I would just love to **do you.**

DONNA
Do me?

SETH
Yes, especially you.

DONNA
No one has ever asked to do me like this before.

SETH
Donna… may I call you Donna?

DONNA
Yes, of course.

SETH
I just want to paint you… a life portrait perhaps… strictly professional.

DONNA
I knew that.

SETH
I don't want to pressure you… here's my card… I have a small studio not far from here.

(She reads the card.)

                    DONNA
Seth... and your phone number... simple and to the point.

                    SETH
Call me.

                    DONNA
Call you? When is a good time?

   (To audience)

He looks like a dork... but's he's smooth... real smooth. I kind of like that.

                    SETH
For you... anytime...

                    DONNA
Okay then,

   (They both look at each other in silence.)

                    SETH
Great to meet you... Venus...

   (Beat.)

Donna.

                    DONNA
Likewise... Seth.

   (Donna holds Seth's card tightly and turns to the audience.)

                    DONNA
I can't believe someone would want to paint me. At first I didn't trust him... he did look a little creepy... but when he said it was strictly professional, I felt better about it. A "life study?" I wonder what that means? If he asks me to take my clothes off... I will definitely refuse... at first... then I'll do it as long as my husband doesn't find out... What am I saying? I can't do this.

(She rips up the card and is about to throw it away.)

                        DONNA
He called me Venus... that was romantic.

(Instead, she holds the pieces in her hand and exits as Seth turns to the audience.)

                        SETH
I can't explain it... but women always fall heavy when you tell them they look like Botticelli's Venus... something about that is always a sure winner. I lied to her about being a painter... it just came out of my mouth... and I went with it. I wanted her to like me... I probably will never see her again... but at that moment in time, I wanted her to like me and think saying I was a painter made me sound more interesting than I really am... I couldn't' help myself... I just did it.

(He laughs to himself and exits.)

#6 DANTE AND THE WAITER
Adapted from the play *Myths and Tangos*

GENDER:	(Male/Female)
AGE RANGE:	(Adult 20's – 50's)
CHARACTERS:	**JOE CLARK** (40'S - 50's) a waiter in a coffee shop who is so much more than he appears to be.
	KIT (20's) a college student.
LOCATION:	A booth in a small coffee shop across from the college campus.
TIME:	The present – Afternoon – after classes.
SYNOPSIS:	Kit a college student, is in love with a guy that won't give her the right time of day. She sits in the coffee shop where he passes by everyday hoping that he'll notice her. Sitting there, she gets advice from an unusual source.
GENRE:	Drama

(Kit turns to audience.)

KIT
Why won't you notice me! Be my lover... my friend and I'll do... I'll be anything you want me to be... without you I am a broken circle... incomplete. Be my lover, my friend and I'll do, I'll be anything you want me to be... I promise.

(Kit turns away and reads a book as Joe enters and stands in front of her.)

JOE
Can I get anything for you?

KIT
I'll have a hot chamomile tea... just bring the water with the bag on the side.

JOE
Anything to go with that?

KIT
No thanks...

(He remains as she goes back to reading.)

JOE
You're doing one of my favorite things to do... just sitting and reading a book.

KIT
Studying...

JOE
Right... I guess you must go to school here?

KIT
Right.

JOE
I used to go to college here myself... but that was a very long time ago.

(Kit returns to reading he tries to see the book title but she covers it.)

JOE
What are you reading about?

KIT
Unrequited love… for English class.

JOE
Lit Crit?

KIT
You got it.

JOE
I think I got a "C" when I took that class. I had a crappy teacher.

KIT
Too bad…

JOE
Yeah it was. You have nice hair.

KIT
Thank you… My boyfriend likes it too.

JOE
Right… better go get your tea.

(He turns to leave, then comes back.)

You don't really have a boyfriend do you?

KIT
Excuse me?

JOE
No boyfriend… am I right?

KIT
What makes you say that?

JOE
You have "**I hope he walks by and notices me**" written all over you.

                    KIT
Do I?

                    JOE
The way you're sitting... anticipating and looking outward as the world goes by... maybe waiting for a special someone to walk by... maybe someone who doesn't even know that you exist... and if they don't notice you... then trying to fill an emptiness that can't be filled... am I right?

                    KIT
What are you a psychic?

                    JOE
No, when you've been around a while... you just know things... call it street smarts... there was a clip on YouTube about it... give me your email... I'll send you the link.

                    KIT
Look, right now all I want is a cup of chamomile tea. Okay?

   (She tries to ignore him standing there... and finally breaks.)

Do you even know what YouTube is?

                    JOE
Why wouldn't I know what YouTube is?

                    KIT
Why would you know YouTube? I mean how old are you?

                    JOE
That's a very personal question to ask someone you hardly know.

                    KIT
Aren't you too old to be looking at YouTube and working here serving coffee? I mean don't people your age have real jobs they go to every day?

JOE
This ***is*** a real job and what does "people my age" mean?

KIT
You know... "Older" like you don't have a clue.

JOE
I'm so sorry I bothered you... I'll get your tea... it's on me.

(She can see that he's genuinely hurt, as he turns to leave, she stops him.)

KIT
Wait... I'm the one who should apologize... I was rude.

JOE
Quite all right... I had it coming.

KIT
What's your name?

JOE
Joe... my name is Joe.

KIT
My name is Kit... short for Catherine. Nice to meet you Joe. Better get back to Dante.

JOE
So ***that's*** what you're reading... Dante.

KIT
Right... Dante... a poem about the love of his life... Beatrice.

JOE
La Vita Nuova... the new life... he wrote about a love he would never have.

                    KIT
Right! He loved her from afar from the first moment he saw.

                    JOE
But Dante could have acted upon it... but he never did... because he was afraid...

                    KIT
He was shy and just a boy... but he loved her all his life until the day he died. She was unattainable... someone he could never get.

                    JOE
We are all obsessed with what is unattainable... truth was... he never acted upon it.

                    KIT
But he couldn't act on it even if he wanted to... he was just a boy. I mean he could never be with her... touch her... kiss her... they were both children... it was a love that was unattainable.

                    JOE
Unattainable is what keeps us longing for more... as long as it's unattainable it stays alive... it's not a bad thing.

                    KIT
It feels like a bad thing... for me now... I feel an emptiness that can't be filled.

                    JOE
The emptiness you feel? Stop fighting it... let it envelope you... once it does, it will vanish and the universe will fill it with the someone you want or someone different and perhaps better... I promise you.

                    KIT
It's just so hard to get through the "now."

                    JOE
As painful as it may seem... accept it.

KIT
Is that what Dante did with Beatrice.

JOE
Something like that... he filled the void with a passion for self improvement and dedicated the rest of his life to perfecting himself so that he would be worthy if he met Beatrice in Heaven... and you know what? He eventually did join her there... for eternity... and that's a lot longer than "now."

KIT
I haven't read that part yet.

JOE
You will... and you're going to be just fine.

KIT
Do you really think I have nice hair?

JOE
I do...

KIT
You really didn't really get a "C" in Lit Crit... did you?

(Beat, he smiles.)

JOE
No... I'll get your tea now.

KIT
Hey Joe... I think I like you... I mean for an old guy...

JOE
Thanks...

(Joe exits as Kit opens her book and smiles.)

#7 MEMORY LANE
Adapted from the play *The Resting Place*

GENDER: (Male/Female)

AGE RANGE: Adult (50's – 60'S)

CHARACTERS: **EDDIE** (50's – 60'S) a retired postal worker who enjoys betting on horses.

FAITH (50's – 60's) Housewife

LOCATION: A Levittown house kitchen in Long Island, New York

TIME: The present – Late morning, with nothing much to do.

SYNOPSIS: An older married couple who are stuck in a boring grey existence reminisce about their past.

GENRE: Drama/Comedy

(OPTIONAL SOUND – ARTIE SHAW'S DANCING IN THE DARK as Faith folds clothes. She sings along and dances as Eddie reads the racing forms.)

FAITH
"Dancing in the Dark... we were dancing in the dark."

EDDIE
Faith, for Christ's sake... give the singing a rest... you're giving me a headache.

FAITH
Why? Singing makes me feel better. You ever try folding clothes? Pretty boring.

EDDIE
That's woman's work.

FAITH
Yeah, right Eddie, that's women's work. Then, what are you good for? I'll tell ya... nothing!

EDDIE
Cut me a break... Can't you see I'm tryin to pick a winner?

FAITH
You couldn't pick a winner out of your nose with your pinky finger.

EDDIE
Is that so?

FAITH
Yeah, that's so...

EDDIE
... and why is that?

FAITH
You really want to do this again?

EDDIE
Yeah, let's take a walk down memory lane... why can't I pick a winner?

FAITH
I'll make this easy... you can't pick a winner because you're a loser... always was... from day one.

(She looks up toward Heaven.)

Why? Why me Jesus? Why did you make me marry this man?

EDDIE
You're sixty years too late Faith... If Jesus was going to help you, he would a done it by now. Sixty years married to the same person...

FAITH
Sixty-three years... I didn't murder anybody... but I feel like I'm living on death row... waiting for the warden to come an get me... clock keeps ticking but he never comes.

EDDIE
That's it Faith... you always hit me when I'm down.

FAITH
Hit you when you're down? You've never been up! What was I thinking when you asked me to marry you? Why did I say yes? I could've had a different life... moved to Hollywood... and maybe been a dancer like Cyd Charisse.

EDDIE
Cut me a break... you were too short to be a dancer... and your ass...

FAITH
Again... you're gonna start on my ass?

EDDIE
I wasn't saying nothing.

FAITH
That's a double negative... you're an idiot...

EDDIE
I'm an idiot and your ass is too big... you could have never been a dancer. Now quit folding clothes and make me a sandwich.

FAITH
I'll make you a sandwich... a nice dry one so you can choke on it!

EDDIE
Then let me choke on it and croak... then you'll be all alone like a dog...

FAITH
Like a dog?

EDDIE
Yeah... like a dog. Why? I'll tell you why... because nobody likes you.

FAITH
I won't be like a dog... people like me.

EDDIE
Okay, name one person.

FAITH
My sister Theresa...

EDDIE
I hate to break it to you... your sister Theresa can't stand you. Why do you think they stopped coming here for the holidays?

FAITH
I thought it was because they didn't like **you**.

EDDIE
Probably that too.

   (Back to racing form)

Here's a winner... **Lovebox Motel...** and he pays 40 to 1...

FAITH
Lovebox Motel? Sounds sexy... you ever think about going to a motel?

EDDIE
Alone?

FAITH
No with me... I mean we could both meet there and pretend...

EDDIE
Pretend what?

FATIH
That we're strangers... on a stormy night... and we have to share one room... like the Clark Gable Claudette Colbert movie... **It Happened One Night**... so romantic.

EDDIE
How are we gonna be strangers? We know everything about each other... sixty-three years... remember. It's different now... not like when we were young.

FAITH
Yeah... those were better days.

EDDIE
You're right about that.

FAITH
You ever think about then... I mean when we were young?

EDDIE
I can't think that far back...

FAITH
Remember the first time we went out. You took me to the Roxy and we saw **Madame X...** it was a murder mystery... you remember now?

EDDIE
A little...

FAITH
After the movie, we walked for an hour and talked... then went to Schlumbaum's on Broadway at Ninety-ninth Street. We shared a banana split...

EDDIE
I kind of remember the banana split.

FAITH
You should, you ate most of it.

EDDIE
Yeah... I guess I did. Those were the good old days.

FAITH
We didn't have a lot but we had it real good back then.

EDDIE
Life was simpler... not like it is now.

FAITH
Much better then... no TV, no Internet... no nothing.

EDDIE
Yeah... no nothing... those were the days.

FAITH
All we had were each other. You were my husky little prince.

EDDIE
...and you were my dancing ballerina.

(Beat. They smile at each other. Then,)

FAITH
You want a tuna sandwich?

EDDIE
Okay... but can I have a little mayo on it?

FAITH
Sure...

EDDIE
...and while you're up there... why don't you sing me that song again.

(Faith exits, then we hear the song.)

FAITH (VO)
Dancing in the Dark... we were dancing in the dark....

(Optional SOUND – ARTIE SHAW'S – DANCING IN THE DARK.)

(Eddie smiles and goes back to reading his racing forms.)

#8 YOU NEVER TELL ME YOU LOVE ME

GENDER:	(Male/Female)
AGE RANGE:	Adult (20's)
CHARACTERS:	**JONATHAN** – a college student in his early twenties, slightly long hair in a tee shirt and jeans.
	BREE – a college student and Jonathan's girlfriend, blonde early twenties sophisticated and impeccably dressed.
LOCATION:	The modestly furnished apartment living room in front of an old television set – not seen.
TIME:	The present – Afternoon.
SYNOPSIS:	You can't always get what you want – The Rolling Stones
GENRE:	Comedy

(OPTIONAL MUSIC – You Can't Always Get What You Want by the Rolling Stones. Jonathan sitting and pointing a remote towards a TV tries to change the channel.)

JONATHAN
Damn! I can get this thing to work.

(Music ends.)

JONATHAN
I'm stuck **Chic and Fabulous** and can't change the channel. This TV has had it.

(Bree enters wearing a dressy dress and sits.)

BREE
That's my favorite show! **Chic and Fabulous** with Designer Dave... let's watch.

JONATHAN
Don't think so... I'm set to watch something else... a documentary.

BREE
Don't tell me... not another UFO documentary?

JONATHAN
Aliens are among us... the truth is out there.

(The remote finally connects and the channel changes.)

Okay, finally... UFO autopsies... I don't think I've seen this one.

BREE
Are you kidding... you've seen it at least ten times. This is the one where they cut up a fake space alien's body... and the green blood looks just like guacamole spread. Really, we've seen this, let's watch something I want to watch for a change.

JONATHAN
I can just hear Designer Dave open the show... **"Dorothy lose the dress... but save the shoes!"** I don't think I could sit through that.

(Bree sits without expression)

JONATHAN
All right Bree... what's up? You okay?

BREE
I'm fine.

JONATHAN
You're fine?

BREE
Yes, fine.

JONATHAN
You don't look fine.

BREE
Jonathan, I said I was fine. So I **am** fine...

(Beat)

As fine as can be expected.

(Jonathan turns back to the TV, then.)

JONATHAN
I knew it! As ***"fine" as can be expected***. Bree Anne what is that supposed to mean? You said, ***"fine as can be expected..."***

BREE
Wait... you just called me by my legal name.

JONATHAN
That **is** your name... Bree Anne?

BREE
You've always called me "Bree" or "Love Bug."

JONATHAN
Bree Anne... you're kidding me right?

BREE
There it is again... ***"Bree Anne..."***

JONATHAN
I just called you **Bree Anne** for emphasis.

BREE
That's what a lawyer would call me...

JONATHAN
All right... I'm sorry... I meant nothing by it.

BREE
Nothing? Why did you say "nothing?" Interesting choice of words... is that where we are... **nothing**? Wow... I didn't see this coming.

JONATHAN
Love bug...

BREE
What?

JONATHAN
I said... **Love bug...**

BREE
A nice gesture but too little too late.

JONATHAN
I called you Love Bug... don't I get any credit for that?

BREE
No credit... all you care about is your television.

JONATHAN
Bree... how can you say that? Can't you see that I'm frustrated with this audiovisual equipment? Have you ever tried to get something to work... and no matter what you did or said... even after you put a lot of time into it.... it just wouldn't work. You try and try... but nothing you do or say matters. After a while you become frustrated and say to yourself... I give up! It's time for something new.

(Beat. Bree is silent then bursts into tears.)

JONATHAN
What the hell did I do now?

BREE
Don't you think I don't know what you're really talking about... ***its time for something new...*** you're breaking up with me!

JONATHAN
Love Bug... I was just talking about getting a new TV.

BREE
Shush... don't say another word... I know... it's been coming for a while now. At first it I thought it was because I got a higher grade than you in Dramatic Lit... it wasn't my fault that Professor Carroll liked my essay more than yours. I wrote both of them!

JONATHAN
You're crazy, you know that?

BREE
...and there's that heinous bitch "Carly Bart" who stares at you in Conversational Italian. Did she really think I couldn't hear her whisper ***"Ciao Jonathan... mi amore?"***

JONATHAN
She never said ***"mi amore."***

BREE
But, that's okay... if you want to be with Carly Bart, that's fine.

JONATHAN
Look, all I want to do is to sit on this couch... relax... and be able to use the a remote to change the channel without getting a cramp in my hand. That's all.

BREE
The truth is... the love is gone between us.

JONATHAN
How can you say such a thing?

BREE
Okay, then, if you love me... how would I know it?

(Beat, he thinks, then...)

JONATHAN
Easy... I washed your car yesterday. Didn't I?

BREE
You're a sly one...

JONATHAN
That's it... I washed your car yesterday... while you stayed in here and did your nails.

BREE
You were outside with your friends drinking beers...

JONATHAN
...and washing your car. Now that's love.

BREE
What about the words Jonathan? The words? You never tell me you love me.

JONATHAN
Okay... Bree... Love Bug... I love you!

(They both sit back.)

BREE
All right... I love you too... Jon Jon...

(Awkward beat.)

JONATHAN
What would you like to do now?

                            BREE
Let's watch TV... together. Let's watch *Chic and Fabulous*... Okay?

   (An insincere smile from Jonathan, then...)

                          JONATHAN
What a great idea.

   (Bree gives him a cold hard stare... until he surrenders the TV remote
   to her. She presses it (it works just fine) sits back, smiles and puts her
   head on Jonathan's s shoulder. He looks forward without expression.)

*Optional VO performed by a third person:

                             VO
Watch out girls... it's time for "Chic and Fabulous! I'm Designer Dave...
"Dorothy lose the dress... but save the shoes!"

#9 BERLIN – DECEMBER 1941
Adapted from the play NIGHTFALL

GENDER: (Male/Female)

AGE RANGE: Adult (20's – 30's)

CHARACTERS: **ANTON KRAUS** - (20's) on leave in Berlin, a young poet who has been drafted into Hitler's Wehrmacht reluctantly finds himself caught up in a world engulfed in war. While there, he runs into his childhood sweetheart – the love of his life.

FRAULINE ERIKA WOLFE - (20's) young, beautiful and an idealized vision of the perfect Arian woman. She walks the fine line between a party faithful and an entitled revolutionary. She is the fiancé of a high ranking Nazi SS officer.

LOCATION: Outside a toyshop window on a busy street in Berlin.

TIME: 1941 – Christmas Eve – Evening

SYNOPSIS: During the Second World War, two childhood friends meet on the streets of Berlin on Christmas Eve. As the war rages around them, the love they had for one another is rekindled.

GENRE: Drama

(OPTIONAL MUSIC - ***Silent Night – German Version –*** as Anton Kraus in a dark suit, watches a model train through a toy store window (not seen. Erika Wolfe, in a coat, appears next to him.)

*Note: Silent Night in German is available on YouTube at https://www.youtube.com/watch?v=aGA6djLsDgs OR an instrumental version is at https://www.youtube.com/watch?v=4NCcqmYCyoQ

                        ERIKA
Aren't you a bit old for toy trains?

                        KRAUS
Never, when I was I boy, I wanted to be a train engineer.

                        ERIKA
I remember.

    (KRAUS looks up and is startled to see Erika.)

                        KRAUS
Wolfe?

                        ERIKA
Yes, Wolfe. My darling poet Anton Kraus!

    (They hug politely.)

                        KRAUS
My childhood sweetheart... Erika Wolfe... what are you doing here?

                        ERIKA
I live here... in Berlin... or have you forgotten?

                        KRAUS
That's right... I knew that. I just can't believe that we have run into each other in such a big city after all these years.

                        ERIKA
I agree... but it seems destiny has willed it... and you promised to write but didn't?

KRAUS
I am sorry for that.

ERIKA
I forgive you.

KRAUS
You must be married to Dieter Esch by now… I remember reading about your engagement in the Cologne papers. I should congratulate you.

ERIKA
We are at war… no time for a wedding.

KRAUS
That sounds like Dieter Esch talking… very practical… he was the same way when we were children.

ERIKA
Dieter… is now SS Hauptsturmführer… stationed just outside of Paris. I am going to be joining him there next month.

KRAUS
Dieter is SS? I'm impressed.

ERIKA
Our families have betrothed us and that will have to be enough for now… but it's my turn… what are you doing in Berlin?

KRAUS
Field Marshal Wilhelm Keitel has ordered me here. I am to report to the French coastline. It seems Herr Hitler wants to build a wall along the entire French coast.

ERIKA
General command? That's very prestigious. But all that doesn't matter right now… what is important is that you are here standing right in front of me!

KRAUS

I am... but Berlin seems different from when we were children.

ERIKA

It was a happier place then. Now, there is a darkness that has fallen upon this city.

KRAUS

Not only Berlin, I have heard rumors about camps... in Poland and Romania.

ERIKA

This is not the Germany we knew. But, it still is our home...

KRAUS

So we just close your eyes and do what we are told? Is that your answer?

ERIKA

Let's not argue... it's been too long. I'm glad you're here... Berlin can be a very lonely place... and I am tired of being alone.

KRAUS

No one should be alone on such a beautiful Christmas night...

ERIKA

In Berlin... we are encouraged not to speak of "Christmas" in favor the winter solstice and Odin... it's the Fuhrer's wish.

KRAUS

For me, it will always be Christmas... the Nazi's can't take that away. Some things will never change... they have always been and will always be.

(Erika has tears in her eyes.)

Wolfe, what's wrong?

ERIKA

You and I... will we change?

KRAUS
We will always be... my dear Erika... no matter what.

(KRAUS is about to kiss her, but is interrupted by **- Air Raid Siren**.)

Allied bombers over Berlin?

*Note Air Raid Siren is available on YouTube at https://www.youtube.com/watch?v=erMO3m0oLvs

ERIKA
Goering boasts the Luftwaffe will shoot the enemy out of the sky and if Allied planes drop bombs on Germany, that we can call him Meyer. I guess his name is Meyer... isn't that funny?

(She laughs then breaks into tears. He comforts her.)

KRAUS
Erika, I have loved you always... since we were children.

ERIKA
...and now?

KRAUS
Forever.

ERIKA
Forever seems such a strange thing to say with bombers flying over our heads? We live our lives on the pointed blade of a dagger... dancing upon its sharpened edge... cheating death... and at any moment we could be cut to shreds.

KRAUS
Wolfe, it's not safe out here... let's go to the shelter... I will stay with you there.

ERIKA
No... I have a better idea... I have a flat near here.

(Erika pulls him closer and kisses him.)

                ERIKA

Do you still write poetry?

                KRAUS

Yes, I do.

                ERIKA

Will you write about tonight?

                KRAUS

If you want me to...

                ERIKA

Good, then come with me...

(They kiss again.)

                ERIKA

I have always loved you more than life itself... Anton Kraus.

                KRAUS

I have always loved you... Erika Wolfe...

(They kiss, again... then.)

...and I will love you until the day I die.

(SOUND AIR RAID SIREN fades as Erika and KRAUS disappear into the darkness. All that remains is the gentle melody of SILENT NIGHT.)

#10 SHAKESPEARE

GENDER:	(Male/Female)
AGE RANGE:	Adult (20's)
CHARACTERS:	**MICHAEL** - a young actor working part time at a movie theatre to pay his rent, give him time to study acting and go on auditions.
	SHAWN STONE – (20's) Michael's part time, actress girlfriend and co-worker. She lives life on the edge - wearing too much make up and too little clothing.
LOCATION:	The empty lobby of the Argo movie theatre just before opening
TIME:	Matinee – afternoon
SYNOPSIS:	Michael and his part time girlfriend Shawn discuss performing a scene from Romeo and Juliet for their acting class.
GENRE:	Comedy

(MICHAEL wearing a dark usher's jacket takes a few minutes to rehearse quietly before the theatre opens.)

MICHAEL

But soft! What light through yonder window breaks? It is the East, and Juliet is the sun!
Arise, fair sun, and kill the envious moon, who is already sick and pale with grief
That thou her maid art far more fair than she.

(Shawn enters in a skimpy outfit and very high heels.)

SHAWN
Aye me...

MICAHEL
That's not right... I still have more lines before you say that.

SHAWN
Sorry.

MICHAEL
Shawn, why aren't you dressed for work? We open in just a few minutes.

SHAWN
Can't...

MICHAEL
What?

SHAWN
Work...

MICHAEL
Why?

SHAWN
I have an audition in a half hour... for a Spike Lemon Drink spot.

MICHAEL
Dressed like that?

SHAWN
I'm supposed to be on the beach.

MICHAEL
You're not wearing a bra?

SHAWN
Do you think it's too over the top?

MICHAEL
More like too little top... I can see right through what you're wearing.

SHAWN
Commercials are so visual... you have to have just the right look or BANG... you're out!

Can you cover for me today?

MICHAEL
Did you tell Beatrice? You know the rules. If you're going to miss your shift, you have to notify management... and that's Beatrice.

SHAWN
I texted her... told her I had food poisoning and was vomiting my brains out...

MICHAEL
Did she write back?

SHAWN
She wanted me to take a selfie and prove it. So, I threw oatmeal and orange juice on the floor and took a picture of it... one must do what one must to be a star.

MICHAEL
So you're good with her?

SHAWN
Not exactly... she wrote back... "**clean up the oatmeal and get your ass in here now or you're fired. LOL**" – Wow... what a buzz kill... I thought she'd be happy I'm going on an audition... But, I'm going no matter what.

MICHAEL
So why are you here?

SHAWN
No Michael, I'm **not** here... get it.

MICHAEL
No you're here... right in front of me.

SHAWN
I need to borrow some money for an Uber... my credit card is maxed out.

MICHAEL
You ever think about hitchhiking? In that get up, you'll get a ride in less than thirty seconds.

SHAWN
Not funny, Michael. Actor to actor... do you consider yourself a supportive person?

MICHAEL
I suppose so...

SHAWN
So, are you going to help me out or what? After all I am almost your girlfriend.

MICHAEL
All I have on me is a twenty...wait... Uber won't take cash?

(He pulls it out and she snaps it away from him.)

SHAWN
I'll take it anyway.

MICHAEL
Can you bring back the change?

SHAWN
Change? Don't think so... I gonna pick up Mocha Grande on my way!

(Beat)

Okay, gotta go!

(She starts to exit.)

MICHAEL
Wait, what about our scene in acting class tonight? We're doing Shakespeare... remember?

SHAWN
I am well aware of that fact.

MICHAEL
Wonderful... have you worked on your lines?

SHAWN
Sure... **"Out spot... out damn spot... I say... I say nay... I say fi"** Something like that...

MICHAEL
Wrong!... What was that?

SHAWN
Shakespeare... can't you tell?

MICHAEL
Can you say it again?

SHAWN
Not now... I am trying to focus on what I have to say for the Spike Lemon Drink spot.

MICHAEL
...and what is that?

SHAWN
...mmmm so deliciously tart...

MICHAEL
That's it?

SHAWN
What were you expecting a monologue? It's a commercial!

MICHAEL
Shawn... we need to rehearse our scene for tonight...

SHAWN
I'm not big on rehearsing... takes away the spontaneity...

MICHAEL
But you don't know your lines? It's Shakespeare!

SHAWN
No worries… we'll improvise! Gotta go!

(Beat, she looks into his eyes with passion)

…mmmm so deliciously tart…

(She fixes her hair, kisses him on the cheek and exits.)

MICHAEL
You can't improvise Shakespeare… someone has got to say the lines.

(Michael sits for a moment then… he goes back to Romeo and Juliet and does both characters.)

Guess I could do both parts…

MICHAEL
(as Juliet)

O Romeo, Romeo! wherefore art thou Romeo?
Deny thy father and refuse thy name;
Or, if thou wilt not, be but sworn my love,
And I'll no longer be a Capulet.

(then as Romeo)

[*Aside.*] Shall I hear more, or shall I speak at this?

(Beat and smiles)

That just might work…

#11 HOT TUB CONFESSION

GENDER: (Male/Female)

AGE RANGE: Adult (20's – 30's)

CHARACTERS: **GEORGE** – (20's – 30's) a young professional stockbroker who is living with Susan over a year in a small midtown apartment. Their relationship is in a holding pattern – not going anywhere.

SUSAN –(20's – 30's) George's girlfriend and recent graduate of NYU Law School – despite the prospect of an exciting career, Susan wants what all of her girlfriends have found – marriage and a family.

LOCATION: Very small midtown apartment in New York City

TIME: Evening

SYNOPSIS: George has come home late again.

GENRE: Drama/Comedy

(SOUND – KNOCK AT THE DOOR.)

GEORGE (OFF)
Susan! It's me... its George! Let me in!

(She opens the door and George in work suit staggers in.)

SUSAN
Why didn't you use your key?

GEORGE
They're in my other suit pocket. Hi.

(He kisses her on the cheek.)

SUSAN
George, you're late again.

GEORGE
It couldn't be helped. I actually planned to leave the office early... but one thing lead to another.

SUSAN
Really?

GEORGE
What is that supposed to mean?

SUSAN
Exactly, what "thing" lead to "another?"

GEORGE
Wasn't exactly a thing... more like a situation... the elevator was out again... took a while to get out of my building.

SUSAN
Ever hear of walking down the stairs?

GEORGE
I did... all twenty-two floors... then I couldn't get a cab. Not one in sight... then I started walking and before I knew it... I had walked all the way home.

SUSAN
That's a good story George... a very good story. It has just the right amount of detail that makes it sound like it **could** be true... but then lacks those smaller details that could if examined... contradict one another... such as... the fact that your shoes are hardly scuffed... not exemplary of a man who has walked over twenty blocks... and then there's that tell tale smell of cheap perfume... almost citrusy... the one your assistant Jeanine

wears... I think they call it **Escada Magnetism**... and if I can smell your breath past the tic tacs you just ingested I would come face to face with the smell of Bombay Sapphire gin with a hint of tonic... am I right?

GEORGE
You are totally off base... Okay... I did stop and have a drink... I'm sorry.

SUSAN
...and I'm supposed to say?

GEORGE
That you forgive me... I'm really sorry... it won't happen again.

SUSAN
I'm not quite sure if I can do that...

GEORGE
I said I was sorry... what do you want from me? I'm telling you're the truth.

SUSAN
No you're not... for once... I would like the real truth.

GEORGE
You want the truth... I'm a good person Susan... I'm a giver... all I do is give... that's the truth.

SUSAN
You're so accustomed to lying, you couldn't tell the truth if you wanted to.

GEORGE
Really? Ask me anything you want... anything and I will tell you the truth.

SUSAN
Nothing but the truth?

GEORGE
Anything.

(Susan thinks for a moment, then...)

SUSAN
Okay... your sister's wedding in the Hamptons.

GEORGE
That again?

SUSAN
You said *"anything."*

GEORGE
I meant anything about today...

SUSAN
No, no no... you specifically said *"anything."* I didn't know anything had a statute of limitations. Okay... at your sister's wedding in the Hamptons you said you spent three hours in the hot tub alone. Looking up at the stars... I think you said.

GEORGE
Let's no go there...

SUSAN
Now the truth... were you really alone in the hot tub looking up at that stars for three hours?

(Beat.)

GEORGE
No.

SUSAN
If you were not *alone*, who was in the said hot tub with you?

GEORGE
I don't remember...

SUSAN
You *do* remember... don't you George... you remember very well.

GEORGE
I had a lot to drink that night... it was dark.

SUSAN
Let me help you refresh your memory... does the name **Abby** ring a bell? She was one of the bride's maids, pretty with long red hair... as I recall she lived in the West Village... you kept calling her **Down Town Abby...** do you remember her now?

GEORGE
No, I don't.

SUSAN
Maybe this will help.

(She flips through her cell phone... to a picture and shows it to him.)

GEORGE
Where did you get this?

SUSAN
Facebook...

GEORGE
You hacked my Facebook account.

SUSAN
Hardly hacked... your password... is "password."

GEORGE
I can't believe you hacked my account... I was just taking a selfie with Abby.

SUSAN
Abby has no top on...can you see that... and those **are** freckled breasts are they not?

(He looks at the picture closely.)

GEORGE
Yes, they appear to be... she probably didn't want to get her clothes wet.

SUSAN
...and there you are with your arm wrapped around her shoulder... smiling and holding one of those freckled breasts...

GEORGE
I wouldn't say holding... more like just touching... brushing against. I can explain...look Susan I'm sorry. I confess to all of it... the hot tub was a mistake... we were all drinking and Abby was an accident... she was only a one-time thing. I confess!

SUSAN
Confession accepted.

GEORGE
Thank you.

   (Beat.)

Wait, that was too easy.

   (Susan flips to another picture on her phone.)

SUSAN
Not "easy" at all... it's just good to get the truth out... **the truth will set you free.**

GEORGE
Okay... so we're good?

SUSAN
Oh... yes we're "good" very "good."

GEORGE
Okay.

SUSAN
George, I also have a hot tub confession to make.

(She shows him the picture on her phone.)

GEORGE

What's this?

SUSAN

This picture is also from your sister's wedding in the Hamptons... actually it was the night after... and here we all are in the same hot tub that you were in the night before with Down Town Abby. In fact... there's Abby right there... you see her?

GEORGE

Right there. We're all dressed and all together... so what's to confess?

SUSAN

Well, you see the guy right next to Abby... he was the "Best Man." His name is Jonathan Kingsman... you remember him? The one with the enormous estate outside of London. Well, here's **my** confession... Jonathan and I have been seeing each other for at least two months now... he's a wonderful man... and you know what George? He's asked me to marry him. Can you beat that? Can you beat that?

(George gets up.)

GEORGE

Well, Susan... I guess that it then?

SUSAN

Yes, George, that's it then... I just love a happy ending... don't you?

GEORGE

I just want you to know Susan... it's not you... it's me.

SUSAN

Not another word... just leave.

(George exits... Susan exits.)

(Beat. George reappears a moment later and hits the speed dial on his cell phone.)

GEORGE

(On phone)

Abby? Georgie... are you still there? My situation has changed... she just broke up with me... saved me the trouble... boy was I relieved... I'll see you in about ten... good. Hey Abby? I just love a happy ending... don't you? Bye.

(George ends the conversation and exits.)

#12 THE FABULOUS JOHNNY ANGEL
Adapted from the play The Fabulous Johnny Angel

GENDER: (Male/Female)

AGE RANGE: Adult (40's – 50's)

CHARACTERS: **JOHNNY ANGEL** – (40's – 50's) an aging lounge singer who performs night after night in an out of the way dive called the TOP HAT LOUNGE.

LILA KATOUR –(30's) a mysterious and sensual woman of consequence. Her short dark hair contrasts her dark red lipstick and matching dress make her look like she's right out of a James Bond movie.

LOCATION: A small stage at the Top Hat Lounge and an empty bar along a long lonely highway going nowhere.

TIME: The Present - late evening

SYNOPSIS: ***The Top Hat Lounge***, on a cold moonlit night. Johnny and Lila sing their last song for the evening and go their separate ways. But on this moonlit night, Johnny just doesn't want to be alone. .

GENRE: Drama/Comedy

(2:00 AM on a cold moonlit night the lounge is empty - the piano we don't see plays EAST OF THE SUN as Johnny and Lily sing.)

*Note the backing track for this song can be found on YouTube at https://www.youtube.com/watch?v=GWfsa7FQGOc&list=RDGWfsa7FQGOc

JOHNN (SINGING)
East of the sun and west of the moon
We'll build a dream house of love dear
Close to the sun in the day - Near to the moon at night
We'll live in a lovely way dear
Sharing our love in the pale moonlight

LILA (SINGING)
Just you and I, forever and a day
Love will not die; we'll keep it that way
Up among the stars we'll find a harmony of life to a lovely tune
East of the sun and west of the moon dear

JOHNY AND LILA
East of the sun and west of the moon

(Instrumental follows as Johnny says goodnight.)

LILA
Thank you for coming out on such a cold night… I'm Lila Katour

JOHNNY
… and I'm The Fabulous Johnny Angel…. we're here at the absolutely fantastic Top Hat Lounge every Wednesday through Saturdays…. And remember…

LILA
"The more you all drink…"

JOHNNY
"The better we sound…" Here's looking at ya!

(He downs a glass of scotch whiskey)

Goodnight!

(Sparse applause... Beat. Johnny and Lila remain on the stage. Johnny turns to a piano player we don't see.)

JOHNNY
Jilly, good job tonight.

(He turns to Lila)

Wow... I'm glad that's over...

LILA
Me too... my feet are killing me... see you tomorrow.

JOHNNY
Lila... wait a minute... why don't you stay and have a drink with me?

LILA
Johnny... I've been having a drink with you all night... actually you've been doing all the drinking... but I've been right up here on stage next to you.

JOHNNY
That's not the same. Come on...

LILA
I'm really tired...

JOHNNY
Come on Lila... then just sit with me a minute.

(Beat. She sits.)

LILA
Johnny what's up?

JOHNNY
I just don't feel like being alone just yet... let's talk.

LILA
I'm sitting... what do you want to talk about?

JOHNNY
It's really cold out there tonight... and the moon is full.

(Beat. They just look at each other.)

LILA
Okay... now that I have the weather report... can I go home? My cat is waiting for me.

JOHNNY
You know sitting here... on a cold night like this with a full moon shining... makes me think of the night we first met. You remember?

LILA
How can I forget... you were singing up there.... and I was sitting right out there...

JOHNNY
And?

LILA
...and you sang to me.

JOHNNY
You remember the song?

LILA
I think it was **I'm in a Sentimental Mood.**

JOHNNY
What did you think?

LILA
I thought... the Fabulous Johnny Angel... was singing a song to me... it was romantic.

JOHNNY
I never thought of myself as romantic.

LILA

Now that I really know you... I would tend to agree... you don't have a romantic bone in your body.

JOHNNY

I'm not sure if that's a compliment.

LILA

It's not... the song was great but when we were together it was hard... very hard.

JOHNNY

I thought we had a lot of fun...

LILA

All the drinking... and the women... not fun.

JOHNNY

I'm sorry... I really am... I wish we could start all over again.

LILA

Let's just forget it okay?

JOHNNY

I can't forget it. I'm a different person now.

LILA

Really? How much scotch did you drink today?

JOHNNY

I don't know... but I've really cut down.

LILA

You've had a drink in your hand all night.

JOHNNY

That? It's just a stage prop. Do I look drunk to you?

(She looks at him closely.)

LILA

Not sure... I can't tell anymore with you... but it really doesn't matter Johnny... it's all water under the bridge.

JOHNNY

Lila, I'd like to cross that bridge again.

LILA

Johnny the bridge is closed... can I go home now?

(She gets up to leave.)

JOHNNY

Wait... you remember this?

(Johnny jumps back up on the stage this is a flash back to when he first met Lila.)

JOHNNY

...and now to wrap it up tonight... one of my favorites. **I'll be Seeing You...**

(A voice out of the darkness.)

LILA

No, don't do that one...

(Piano continues softly in the background. Johnny looks out into the audience.)

JOHNNY

Excuse me?

LILA

Why don't you do **I'm in a Sentimental Mood?**

JOHNNY

I already sang that tonight. Would you like me to do it again?

LILA

I would… and try to remember the lyrics this time. If not, I can sing it for you.

JOHNNY

Okay…

(Johnny extends his arm outward and invites Lila on the stage.)

JOHNNY

Have met before?

LILA

No…

JOHNNY

You got a name?

LILA

Yeah sure… Lila… Lila Katour

JOHNNY

Hello, Lila… I think I just fell in love.

(Johnny steps back down and sits next to Lila.)

You remember that?

LILA

Yeah, I do.

JOHNNY
...after all this time. That's a good thing... right?

LILA
Yeah... it's a good thing... and then we sang the song.

(Soft piano plays **"I'm in a Sentimental Mood."**

Note: Backing track available on YouTube: https://www.youtube.com/watch?v=6MvaB7NQo3g

JOHNNY
We sang it together for the first time.... in the key of "C." Which was a little high for me.

LILA
Not for you... you were **The Fabulous Johnny Angel**...

(The draw closer together and she kisses him.)

JOHNNY
Why'd you do that?

LILA
Just curious...

JOHNNY
Do you want to do it again?

LILA
It did cross my mind...

(She kisses him again. As they do, SOUND soft piano playing **I'm in a Sentimental Mood** plays and they smile at one another.)

#13 THE GOOD SAMARITAN

GENDER: (Male/Male)

AGE RANGE: Adult (20's – 40's)

CHARACTERS: **DETECTIVE BLACK** – (20's – 40's) a Metro Police Detective that's caught somewhere between good cop and bad cop...

SIMON STONE –(20's – 40"s) a helpful neighbor who is providing information voluntarily to assist Detective Stone in identify a suspect in a robbery/homicide case.

LOCATION: Interrogation room #4 at the Metro Precinct.

TIME: The Present – afternoon

SYNOPSIS: Simon Stone has been coming in on a regular basis providing information to Detective Black toward the solving of a burglary turned homicide in the neighborhood.

GENRE: Drama

(BLACK sits at a table across from STONE.)

BLACK
Thanks for coming back in again today.

STONE
No problem... anything I can do to help.

                    BLACK
Great… because Mr. Stone… I don't know where we'd be without **Good Samaritans** like you… this case really has us stumped.

   (Beat)

Mrs. Felker is not the first senior citizen to be robbed… but she is the first to be killed during a robbery. Someone must have followed her into her apartment, then strangled her… with some sort of rope or wire… we haven't found it yet.

                    STONE
I think it's terrible… the amount of violence there is all around us today.

                    BLACK
It is a dangerous world out there… so you're saying that the guy you saw in the alley way was definitely black?

                    STONE
African American… About six feet tall, blue sweatshirt, black pants and sport shoes.

                    BLACK
Sneakers?

                    STONE
Yes…

                    BLACK
Did you see his face?

                    STONE
No, he was walking away from me… I only saw the back of his head.

                    BLACK
How did you know he was black? African American?

   (Beat)

STONE
His hair... he had a black man's hair.

BLACK
Okay, and you saw this yesterday?

STONE
Early evening... about six.

BLACK
Okay... and you were in the alleyway as well... walking your dog?

STONE
Yes...

STONE
I bet you see a lot of things when you walk a dog... people's comings and goings... habits... things like that.

STONE
I guess so.

BLACK
What made the African American stand out to you?

STONE
He's wasn't from the neighborhood... I'd never seen him before.

BLACK
What was he doing? I mean was he just walking or getting out of a car?

STONE
No... just walking... first slow... looking around... then faster after he turned and saw me walking toward him.

BLACK
So he started to walk away from you "faster" after he saw you walking your dog?

STONE

Yes.

BLACK

Did you see his face when he turned back and saw you?

STONE

I told you I didn't see his face...

BLACK

Right... how far away would you estimate he was when you saw him turn toward you and then walk away?

STONE

I don't know...I'm not sure.

BLACK

Ten yards... twenty... thirty?

STONE

Thirty...maybe more.

BLACK

...and you could tell that he was an African American from that distance?

STONE

I told you I wasn't sure. All I know is that he was "black" and not from the neighborhood.

BLACK

African American... isn't the alleyway pretty dark by six. You'd have to have excellent vision to spot a black man in the dark from thirty yards... wouldn't you say?

STONE

I wouldn't.

BLACK

Right.

STONE
Well, I have to be going now... I hope I was of some help.

BLACK
Yes, Mr. Simon... thank you...

STONE
You're welcome.

(Stone gets up to leave, when Black stops him.)

BLACK
Oh, Mr. Simon... one more thing...

STONE
Of course...

BLACK
Have you ever met Mrs. Felker?

(Beat.)

STONE
Mrs. Felker? No... No I haven't.

BLACK
That's funny... because when I said her name... you acted as if you knew exactly who I was talking about.

STONE
Nope...

BLACK
I thought maybe you might of met her when you were walking your dog... you might have run into her as she was coming home from her Tuesday reading club... she was murdered on a Tuesday... did you know that? I'm thinking she knew her killer... and maybe it was someone she felt comfortable letting into her house... have you ever been in Mrs. Felker's house?

STONE
No... I have not. I'd like to stay Detective Black but I really should be going.

BLACK
To walk your dog?

STONE
She's been locked up in my apartment all day... I should take her for a walk.

BLACK
Right... when you walk your dog... do you walk her on a leash?

STONE
Of course...

BLACK
Is the leash red?

STONE
More like Crimson...

BLACK
Crimson? That's red isn't it?

STONE
I suppose so.

BLACK
You know that's funny... the CSU unit found red residue around Mrs. Felker's neck... it appears she was strangled with something that was red... maybe like a red leash.

(Beat.)

STONE
That comment sounds accusatory... are you implying that I strangled Mrs. Felker?

BLACK

No, just asking for your help Mr. Stone... to help... isn't that what you like to do? You like to help?

STONE

All I was trying to do was be a *Good Samaritan*...

BLACK

I understand.

STONE

That's the trouble today... no one trusts anyone anymore... no one helps anyone anymore? All I want to do help people! Can't you understand that?

BLACK

I do... I really do.

STONE

I want a lawyer.

BLACK

Mr. Stone... I thought you wanted to help me?

STONE

I'm done helping you... I said I want a lawyer.

BLACK

Okay, Mr. Stone... we're going to have to do this the hard way.

STONE

I have nothing to hide.

(BLACK turns his attention a mirrored wall (the audience.)

BLACK
This "Good Samaritan" wants a lawyer.

#14 THE LIBRARY

GENDER: (Female/Female)

AGE RANGE: Adult (Teens)

CHARACTERS: **STACEY** – (Teen) the locomotive

RHONDA –(Teen) the caboose.

LOCATION: Library at school

TIME: The Present – afternoon

SYNOPSIS: Stacey and Rhonda are best friends would rather be anywhere than sitting in the library waiting for the last bell.

GENRE: Comedy

STACEY
OMG… Rhonda, are you actually reading a book?

RHONDA
I'm just staring at the pages… don't they have any books on the study list with pictures?

STACEY
No

RHONDA
Where's your tablet?

STACEY
I was late this morning and forgot it.

RHONDA
Not good...

STACEY
Not good. What are you reading?

(Rhonda flips through her phone.)

RHONDA
Nylon... Kanye's at it again... how can anyone be married a person like that?

(Beat.)

STACEY
You think you would ever get married?

RHONDA
To a guy?

STACEY
No to a Bassett Hound... of course a guy!

(An OFF SHUSH cuts Rhonda's laugh short.)

RHONDA
Sorry...

(turns back to Stacey)

Stacey... as you are my best friend since first grade... I will tell you the truth... **not a chance!** I can't even get anyone to ask me to the prom.

STACEY
Why not?

RHONDA
Nobody likes me...

STACEY
Get off it!

(OFF SHUSH, then quietly)

Sorry... What about Jimmy Honda?

RHONDA
Really? So everybody will call me Rhonda Honda.... I don't think so... besides Jimmy's got yellow teeth.

STACEY
Really?

RHONDA
Yep... when you get up real close to him... his teeth are yellow... kind of filmy... grosses me out.

STACEY
Gross.

RHONDA
You know it... what time is it?

STACEY
Ten to three...

RHONDA
Ten more minutes of this torture and then we're out of here.

STACEY
Who ever thought up "study period" in the library anyway? Nobody studies... ever.

RHONDA

I just think they do it to screw with us... What about you... are you going to the prom?

STACEY

No offers...

RHONDA

What about... Gerald Spacey?

STACEY

No way... so they can call me **Stacey Spacey**...

RHONDA

I didn't think of that...

STACEY

He's nice too... but doesn't have a car... the thought of his parents driving us to the prom definitely puts Gerald on the **"no go"** list.

RHONDA

Right... what about this idea? We can go together?

STACEY

You mean like prom dates?

RHONDA

OMG! Fabulous idea!

STACEY

Let's do it!

(They slap hands and are shushed again. Both turn in unison to the shush.)

STACEY/RHONDA

Sorry... really sorry.

(They are harshly shushed again.)

Actually... Bite me! Bite Us...

(They both laugh and go back to their reading.)

#15 HAUNTED

GENDER:	(Female/Male)
AGE RANGE:	Adult (Twenties)
CHARACTERS:	**CYNDI BARNES** – (20's) an amateur parapsychologist who is actually terrified of ghosts but finds herself drawn to the spirit world.
	SOTO – (20's Male) a pale-faced nerdish tech type who Cyndi met the day before at a coffee shop has offered to accompany her to a house she believes is haunted.
LOCATION:	A dilapidated and abandoned Victorian Mansion.
TIME:	Just before midnight.
SYNOPSIS:	CYNDI has received an anonymous tip about the house and she and SOTO set out to document the phenomena.
GENRE:	Drama

(Cyndi and Soto walk slowly into the house as a HEAVY BREATHING SOUND reverberates through the house.)

                    CYNDI
Soto, did you record that?

(Soto checks a sensor in his cell phone.)

SOTO
I'm picking it up right now... not to worry.

CYNDI
It's a moaning sound... I want to document as much as we can and then leave.

SOTO
You're a parapsychologist don't you want to find out?

CYNDI
I'm a parapsychologist who receives an anonymous note to come to this house at midnight... don't you think that's a little strange all by itself?

SOTO
No... I think it's compelling... I think we should stay until midnight.

CYNDI
I have a bad feeling about his place. Let's take a few pictures and readings than get the hell out of here. We should come back with a full crew.

SOTO
Cyndi... that's why I'm here... remember?

(Soto takes a few shots with his phone when Cyndi stops in her tracks.)

CYNDI
What was that?

SOTO
I'm sorry I didn't hear anything.

CYNDI
I did... it was that same moaning sound... almost like someone asleep or waking up.

SOTO
I didn't pick up anything.

CYNDI
Look, I've seen all I have to see... let's just stay where we are... take a few more pictures and hit the road.

SOTO
Whatever you say...

CYNDI
What time is it?

(Soto checks a pocket watch.)

SOTO
Almost midnight.

CYNDI
Great... that's funny, you carry a pocket watch... I feel like I've seen it before.

SOTO
...an old habit.

CYNDI
Let's just sit right here for a moment... I feel comfortable right here. I feel like I've been here before.

SOTO
This is a parlor... and right there were two soft chairs... and a settee over there by the window...

CYNDI
... and right there... a mahogany table... with an alabaster bowl on it.

SOTO
Yes, that's right.

CYNDI
The bowl was used for calling cards when people came to visit... if we were not home....

SOTA

Yes...

CYNDI

...they would leave their card. How would I know that?

SOTO

A vision of the past can often be a window into the future.

(The two of them just sit there in silence, then.)

CYNDI

What time is it?

SOTO

Almost midnight.

CYNDI

Sorry. I know this is kind of a strange question to ask... considering where we are and everything... but... do you believe in ghosts?

SOTO

That is not a yes or no answer...

CYNDI

What does that mean?

SOTO

It means that what you are referring to as a ghost is actually a manifestation of the spirit world... spirits can exist in many forms both spiritual and living realm. Depends upon what brings the spirit forward.

CYNDI

Why would a spirit need to manifest itself?

SOTO

Perhaps there is unfinished business here in the living realm.

CYNDI

What would you consider "unfinished business?"

SOTO
Maybe an untimely death... they were taken away before it was time.

(SOUND OF A MOAN.)

CYNDI
There it is again... I really need to leave...

SOTO
Just a moment more...

(Cyndi gets up to leave.)

CYNDI
Sorry, I'm outta here.

(Cyndi starts out... and is stopped in her tracks when she hears a clock strike midnight.)

(*Note: Clock strike is available on YouTube at https://www.youtube.com/watch?v=7lj1nvkY6ks)

SOTO
There... it is midnight... all is again as it should be.

CYNDI
What does that mean?

SOTO
It means that I can leave now.

CYNDI
Great, let's go...

SOTO
No, you must remain.

CYNDI
Why would I want to do that?

SOTO

It is your destiny...

CYNDI

My destiny?

SOTO

You have returned home...

CYNDI

This is not my home...

SOTO

It was in the past... you lived here and died within these very walls.

CYNDI

Who the hell are you?

SOTO

You don't remember me... I lived here as well... Soto... I was your butler... you were just a child.

CYNDI

Soto... I remember that name somehow.

SOTO

You were born in this house... you played right there under the window... as a little girl... and it was in this house that your spirit was untimely separated from your body.

CYNDI

I died here?

SOTO

Cholera... you fought it valiantly and until you drew your last breath... but you would not accept it... and your spirit lived on... it has inhabited many mortals since then... it has taken me quite a long time to find you... but now it's time for you to be rejoined... and move on. Be at peace...

CYNDI
Look this is all very creepy... I'm going home now.

SOTO
You are home.

CYNDI
This creepy place is not my home....

SOTO
You are buried within these walls...

CYNDI
...and that sound?

SOTO
You... it has always been you...

CYNDI
Well, I don't want it to "be" me!

(Cyndi tries to leave but something draws her back.)

What's holding me back?

SOTO

You...   CYNDI
Soto, I don't want to all alone here...

SOTO
You will never be alone... ever again.

(Soto exits.)

CYNDI
Soto...

(Cyndi closes her eyes and begins to breath heavily as if she is out of breath. Her breathing increases in intensity until she exhales one long last breath, closes her eyes and falls into a peaceful calm.)

#16 HOME SWEET HOME
Adapted from the play *The Resting Place*

GENDER: (Male/Female)

AGE RANGE: Adult (30's to 50's)

CHARACTERS: **JOEY FANELLI** – (20'S - 30's) – a successful businessman who has lost his way. He feels empty and his life has no meaning.

FAITH FANELLI – (50's – 60's) Joey Fanelli's Mother who is like a rose, beautiful and thorned all at the same time.

LOCATION: Living Room of Joey's childhood home, Franklin Square, New York

TIME: Late Afternoon

SYNOPSIS: After not speaking to her for many years since his father's death, Joey decides to take the red eye from Los Angeles to his childhood home to see his mother in Long Island, New York after getting word that she is dying.

GENRE: Comedy

(Joey has go through the front window to get into his house because his mother FAITH is motionless on the couch with a magazine over her head.)

JOEY
(Quietly)

Ma?

(No answer... he fears the worst and approaches her tentatively)

Ma...

(Still no answer. Then he loses it.)

MA!

FAITH
(From under the magazine.)

What are you trying to do? Wake up the dead? Can't you see I'm trying to take a little nap here?

JOEY

Hello, ma.

FAITH

Who are you?

(They look at each other long and hard.)

JOEY

It's Joey... your son.

FAITH

Son? I have no son... the only son I had left me like a dog to go live in Los Angeles.

JOEY

Ma... cut the crap...

FAITH

I'm having a moment... can't I even have a moment?

JOEY

Okay... have your moment.

(Beat.)

FAITH

Forget it... the moment is gone.

JOEY

I'm here because I got a call from your doctor saying you were in the hospital...

FAITH

...and now I'm back home...

(Faith sits up slowly then Joey sits next to her and hugs her tentatively. She starts to cry then catches herself.)

JOEY

Ma... I was worried about you.

FAITH

I have to be in the hospital with tubes in my nose for you to worry...

(He squeezes her tighter.)

Not so hard, I bruise like a grape.

JOEY

Are you okay?

FAITH

Of course I'm okay... they got a pill for everything today... they can keep you alive even after you're dead.

JOEY

I got scared... the way you were laying there... I thought you were...

FAITH

Go ahead... say it.

JOEY
Sleeping.

FAITH
You meant *dead*.

JOEY
I never said *dead*.

FAITH
You didn't say *dead* but you thought dead...

JOEY
Well... just for a split second.

FAITH
Don't worry... I'll give you notice before I croak so you can make sure it can fit into your schedule.

JOEY
Ma... I can't help it if I'm busy... living in LA is like living in the fast lane.

FAITH
If you ask me, LA is a pit!... all those earthquakes... LA you can have it. Help me up.

(Joey helps her get up. As she does... she sings the Arlo Guthrie song.)

"Coming in to Los Angelees... bringing in a coupla... keeeys... and my son lives out there with all the palm trees... because he really doe's care about me..."

JOEY
Ma... I had long flight... do we have to do this.

FAITH
This? This is what I do... you want me to drop everything because you show up?

JOEY
The doctor said you had a stroke.

FAITH
A "Minnie stroke." Just like the mouse...

JOEY
Funny, when he told me "Minnie..." I thought the same thing... Minnie Mouse... but a stroke is a serious thing. So I took the red eye into JFK... make sure you're all right.

FAITH
What are you a doctor now?

JOEY
No, I just want to make sure there's someone here to take care of you. You're all alone.

FAITH
Don't worry... I won't bother you... I'm not alone... I have friends to take care of me.

JOEY
Who? Sheila from Second Avenue?

FAITH
Maybe...

JOEY
You **hate** Sheila.

FAITH
It's not nice to say the word **hate.** I don't hate Sheila even though she's a leach...that sucks the marrow right out of my bones! That's not hate.

JOEY
...okay what about the lady down the street? What's her name Mrs. Fabrizio?

FAITH
Mary? She watches soap operas all day... she's an idiot.

JOEY
How about Lucy?

FAITH
Lucy Paretti?

JOEY
Yeah, you two were very close.

FAITH
Not any more... she's stuck in Boca... that's in Florida.

JOEY
I know where Boca is... how's she doing?

FAITH
Not so good... she died last year.

JOEY
She's dead? You said she was in Boca?

FAITH
I said "stuck" in Boca... that's where she's buried... with all the friggin swamps and crocodiles... can you imagine that?

JOEY
She was your best friend... I'm so sorry.

FAITH
Whatever...

JOEY
Didn't you like her?

FAITH
Of course I liked her... what's wrong with you?

JOEY

What did I say now?

FAITH

How can I not like her... she's dead. You can't be disrespectful of the dead.

JOEY

Okay, when she was alive... did you like her?

FAITH

Alive?

JOEY

Alive.

FAITH

She got her hair done twice a week. Who needs their hair done twice a week? Could you like someone like that?

JOEY

The truth is you never got along with anyone. It's your personality.

FAITH

Go ahead... that's it. Put a dagger in me! Yes, a dagger plunged right in my heart!

JOEY

(laughs)

A dagger in your heart? Wow...

FAITH

You think I sound funny?

JOEY

No, I think you sound like Shakespeare.

FAITH

That's it Mr. Comedian.... Go ahead... why don't you twist the blade another inch!

JOEY

Ma, come on… I'm sorry.

(He hugs her.)

FAITH

Famous last words… you feel thin… you should eat something… I'll make you a tuna sandwich.

JOEY

Jesus… Ma, please no tuna… I'm okay.

FAITH

Nonsense! Have a tuna sandwich. You're home now… **HOME SWEET HOME!**

(Faith exits as Joey sits and let's out a sigh.)

#17 THE HAPPY HOUR

GENDER: (Male/Female)

AGE RANGE: Adult (20's – 30's)

CHARACTERS: **JANE** (20's -30's) – A successful businesswoman – VP of marketing at the firm where she works who seemingly has it all.

GLADYS (20's – 30's) - A retail store manager, poor and barely able pay her bills every month.

LOCATION: An Industrial-chic cocktail bar in midtown Manhattan.

TIME: Happy Hour

SYNOPSIS: Two good friends meet at a neighborhood Happy Hour every Friday night, before heading home.

GENRE: Comedy

(Both Jane and Gladys sit side by side sipping Lemon Kamikazes.)

JANE
Cheers.

GLADYS
Cheers…

(They simultaneously drink.)

JANE

That was good.

JANE

Excellent... I love coming to happy hour...

(To a bartender we don't see.)

Two more Lemon Kamikazes... Jack.

GLADYS

I'll second that...

(Beat.)

GLADYS

How was the office today?

JANE

Same crap... different day... they're doing some sort of quarterly review... they want my numbers in by next Friday.

GLADYS

You have numbers?

JANE

I have a lot of numbers... and none of them seem to add up. What about you?

GLADYS

Pretty much the same... in retail you're in a perpetual state of inventory. The new Fall line comes in next week and we have to see what's still in the inventory from summer... and then move it all out with a big sale.

JANE

Count me in!

GLADYS

Forget it... the merchandise is crappy... and too expensive to start with. So it's not really a sale.

JANE
What are you going to do?

GLADYS
Simple... I'll do the inventory and then let management figure out how to move it all out... what about you?

JANE
What about what?

GLADYS
Your quarterly thing... the numbers?

JANE
Hmmm... let me see... I'm going to pull those numbers right out of my ass...then put those numbers in columns...add them up... and then send them out by Friday.

GLADYS
Aren't you afraid you'll get caught?

JANE
No... and if I do... I don't care.

GLADYS
But you might get fired... you're a Vice President... you make a lot of money.

JANE
Not that much... after taxes... and all I do is work... ten hour days... by the time I get home... the only energy I have left is to take off my make up and fall face first right into my bed.

GLADYS
Pretty much the same here... retail is a life fucker... all I do is work... except I don't make the money you do. I hate my life.

JANE
I hate my life more...

(Gladys holds up her glass.)

GLADYS
Let's drink to that...

JANE
I'm in... to hating our lives!

(The finish off their drinks just as two new drinks arrive.)

GLADYS
Thanks Jack...

(Aside to Jane.)

You think Jack is married?

JANE
No... too young.

GLADYS
He's cute...

JANE
If you like that kind of metro sexual... look... I thin tie, worn with open collar just so and the pastel shirt always tucked in to that thin pencil waste line and his shirt sleeves uniformly folded back so that the reach the same exact spot in his forearms.

GLADYS
Wow... you could be a detective...

JANE
Ya 'know... Jack just might be gay...

(In unison, they both look over at the bartender (OFF) as he moves past them.)

JANE
Just might.

GLADYS
Have you been doing any dating lately?

JANE
Low blow Gladys... low blow... You went right from "gay" to dating... and I know that's because of Paul. I only went out with Paul three times before he told me... well actually he texted me... I hardly had enough time to truly investigate his sexual orientation.

GLADYS
You only went out with him three times?

JANE
That's all, but I suspected. It was the little things... like when he kept singing musical theatre songs to himself when we were walking in the park.

(The sip their drinks simultaneously as they look around the room in unison then put their glasses down.)

GLADYS
Jane, there is something I have to tell you.

JANE
What's that?

GLADYS
...about Paul.

JANE
What about Paul?

GLADYS
He's not gay...

JANE
How would you know that?

GLADYS
I've been dating him... maybe three weeks now. He's not gay...

JANE
Well... that's what he said in his text message.

GLADYS
I know... he just wanted to cut it off with you.

JANE
He told you that?

GLADYS
Yes... he just couldn't figure another way.

JANE
He could have just told me... or do what every other guy does... just not call me back.

GLADYS
I'm sorry... I should have told you sooner.

JANE
You should have...
    (Beat.)

But I forgive you.

GLADYS
So we're good?

JANE
We're good... I wouldn't miss our "Happy Hours" for anything.

GLADYS
I feel the same way... let's drink to that.

JANE

I'm in!

(They raise their glasses and toast.)

GLADYS/JANE

To Happy Hours!

(They both smile at one another... then put their glasses down in unison, then look at the men in the room like lions hunting in the Serengeti. Gladys quietly begins to hum then sing a show tune from the musical "Chorus Line"... **"Kiss today goodbye... and point me toward tomorrow."**)

#18 THE SPILT

GENDER: (Male/Female)

AGE RANGE: Adult (30's)

CHARACTERS: **HOLLY** – (30's) – Michael's girl friend of six months.

MICHAEL - (30's) - Holly's boy friend of six months.

LOCATION: "The Split." a trendy upscale restaurant in the heart of town.

TIME: Evening

SYNOPSIS: The couple decides to celebrate their six-month anniversary by going out to a nice restaurant. Holly and Michael are sitting at an empty table each reading a menu.

GENRE: Comedy

HOLLY
I've heard so much about this place.

MICHAEL
From?

HOLLY
Who else? Janet...

MICHAEL
Holly, are we talking about the same Janet that recommended **The Stinking Rose?**

HOLLY
How was I supposed to know every dish was made of garlic? Michael... tell the truth... we did have a great time that night... and the atmosphere was really nice.

MICHAEL
I wouldn't know... my eyes were burning so much from the garlic I had to keep them closed most of the night... and I still can't wear my blue linen shirt I had on that night... still smells like a Garlic sandwich... at least it will keep the vampires away.

HOLLY
Come on... Janet was only trying to be nice... that's why she thought this place would be the perfect choice for our six-month anniversary.

MICHAEL
I just want to remind you when we went on our first double date with her... Janet made a hundred dollar bet with me that we wouldn't last six months. Her boyfriend Dave was the witness.

HOLLY
Dave and Janet have broken up...

MICHAEL
Not totally broken... they're still friends... and as far as I know the bet is still on.

HOLLY
There's was no **real** bet... Janet was only making a joke...

MICHAEL
Really? Why didn't anybody laugh then? Why wasn't Dave laughing?

HOLLY
I think Dave laughed... but he just laughed quietly. Now can't we just put all that behind us and enjoy our anniversary dinner?

MICHAEL
Fine with me.

HOLLY
Okay... whatever you say... Let's figure out what we're going to have.

MICHAEL
I can't believe they haven't even set our table... or brought us some water. I'm going to mention that on Yelp... what's the name of this place again?

HOLLY
"The Split..."

MICHAEL
The Spilt? That's the name of this restaurant?

HOLLY
Yes.

MICHAEL
So, Janet recommended we go out for our six-month anniversary at a restaurant called "The Split?"

HOLLY
Yes, she did...

MICHAEL
Don't you see what's happening here? This is a set up... Janet purposely recommended a restaurant that she knew would be horrible... because she wants us to have a fight... and break up... Janet wants us to break up before the six months are up... so she can win the hundred-dollar bet!

HOLLY
Michael, you're being ridiculous... Janet is my best friend... always will be... She probably doesn't even remember the bet.

MICHAEL
Really? Let's call her.

HOLLY
I'm **not** going to call her... let's end this conversation now!

MICHAEL
Okay... fine with me.

(Michael let's out a frustrated sigh.)

HOLLY
What are we having?

(They both stare at the menus for a long while. Michael breaks the silence.)

MICHAEL
I wonder if anyone will ever come to this table... not a knife, a fork, a napkin... not to mention a glass of water... nothing... not even a...

(Holly cuts him off.) HOLLY

What are you thinking of having?

MICHAEL
I can't make up my mind...

HOLLY
So you don't even know what you want yet? So if a waiter **did** come... we'd have to send him away because you're not ready.

MICHAEL
I **am** ready... I just haven't made up my mind.... between two maybe three things... and I'm sure there are "specials" we don't even know about?

HOLLY
Specials?

MICHAEL
Yes, "special" dishes prepared by the chef that aren't on the menu... I guess you're not used to eating in a finer dining establishments... because in finer restaurants they have specials.

HOLLY
Are you insinuating that I don't know what a "special" is?

MICHAEL
Well?

HOLLY
I don't like your tone!

MICHAEL
My tone? All you've done since we got here… is to protect your stupid "BFF" Janet and disagree with everything I say?

HOLLY
I disagree with you because the things you say are paranoid and stupid.

MICHAEL
So, now I'm paranoid and stupid? There it is… you're probably in cahoots with Janet!

HOLLY
In cahoots with what?

MICHAEL
You know **what**… the bet. The hundred dollars!

HOLLY
You're accusing me to trying to cheat you out of a crappy hundred dollars? What a cheap paranoid asshole… I'm outta here!

(Holly gets up and storms out as Michael calls after her.)

MICHAEL
Cheap?

HOLLY
Yes, cheap! Janet said you'd never pay up…

MICHAEL
I knew it! You can tell Janet I'm not paying a dime!

(Beat. Michael now alone goes back to looking at the menu.)

Let's see… chicken looks good… but I'll wait to choose after I hear the specials.

#19 THE WINDOW JOB

GENDER:	(Male/Female)
AGE RANGE:	Adult (30's – 40's)
CHARACTERS:	**JASON STYLES** – (40's male) – a recent graduate of college with a degree in philosophy who is in desperate need of employment.
	MS. UMA KALE (30's – 40's) a rather uptight corporate type dressed in a business suit. She's a Human Resources specialist at a department store. Her only friend in the world is her cat.
LOCATION:	Human Resources Office
TIME:	Early Morning
SYNOPSIS:	Jason is interviewing for a job as a window decorator at a major department store. He is just out of college, has no experience but needs a job badly.
GENRE:	Comedy

(Ms. Kale with pad and pen greets Jason as he enters her office.)

KALE
Mr. Styles... good morning.

JASON
Morning Ms.... Kale.

(They sit.)

KALE
It's "KAH" "LAY." Everyone just assumes because it is spelled K A L E that it's Kale... but that's neither here nor there... Mr. Style. Let's get right to it.

JASON
Right, I apologize Ms. Ka Lay.

KALE
Yes of course... accepted. Now are you wondering why we are having this *face à face so* early in the morning? Our store hasn't opened yet.

JASON
I just figured you wanted to get an early start.

KALE
Partially correct Mr. Styles... I also wanted to see if you could be in attendance bright and early... and ready to go.

JASON
Yes, that's me... ready to go.

KALE
Excellent... I see you attended college.

JASON
Graduated.

KALE
...with a degree in Philosophic studies.

JASON
I did...

KALE
Not much demand for a philosopher... I would imagine.

JASON
Well actually at some point, I was thinking about law school.

KALE
Law?

JASON
Yes, the philosophy of law and jurisprudence that studies basic questions about law and legal systems, such as "what is law?", "what are the criteria for legal validity?", "what is the relationship between law and morality?", and many other similar questions.

KALE
Really? All French to me I'm afraid… now let's get down to brass tacks shall we?

JASON
Absolutely…

KALE
Do you have any experience in woman's fashion?

(Beat… he doesn't know how to answer this.)

Let me put it another way… do you know how to **dress** in women's clothing?

JASON
Are you asking me if I routinely wear woman's clothing?

KALE
No, of course not… I'm asking if you know how to dress a woman… more specifically a mannequin?

JASON
I think I could dress a mannequin.

KALE
Mr. Styles… you are aware that this job… the one you are applying for is to work with our merchandising staff, select appropriate garments… accessories and dress the mannequins in our store windows… and on occasion within the store.

JASON
Wow… all that "dressing" sounds like a lot of fun.

KALE
Fun it may be… but can you do it? Or shall I say have you done it?

(Beat.)

I need complete honesty.

JASON
Well, Ms. Kah Lay... I've **undressed** a few woman when I was in college... I mean not a lot of women... but a few. I can list them for you on my resume?

KALE
Mr. Styles... a personal answer is not required.

JASON
I mean, how hard can it be? You pull a zipper down to take something off, unclip a clasp... it's pretty much the same thing in reverse... wouldn't you think?

KALE
Mr. Styles... I don't know what to think.

JASON
Look, what I don't have in experience... I certainly have in enthusasm.

KALE
I would agree with you there.

JASON
You can also check my transcripts... I have a 4.0 GPA... I worked hard in school and I will work hard here. Just give me a chance!

KALE
Mr. Styles... you drive a hard bargain. But I'm afraid I am going to have to say no... we truly require someone with the **appropriate** experience. I'm so sorry.

(Beat.)

Good day... Mr. Styles.

(Beat. Kale extends her hand to shake his. He does the same and shakes her hand. Then without warning he leans over the desk, gently caresses Kale's face and kisses her on the lips.)

JASON

I hate the word **appropriate...**

(Jason turns and quietly leaves Kale's office. Then, she calls out to him.)

KALE

Mr. Styles!

(Jason pops his head right back again in the door of her office.)

You may start tomorrow at 7:30 AM... sharp!

JASON

Thank you.... Mrs. Kah Lay... I won't let you down...

(Jason exits. Ms. Kale shakes her head and smiles to herself as she makes a notation on her pad.)

#20 THE END

GENDER:	(Male/Male)
AGE RANGE:	Adult (30's – 40's)
CHARACTERS:	**MARTIN NELSON** – (30's – 40's) a history professor at a local community college and a part time novelist. He was married for a short time but his wife left him. All he has now is a modest house and a small dog.
	DAMON RAVEN (30's – 40's) a funeral counselor at Eternal Lawns Memorial Park wearing a dark conservative suit carrying a small folder.
LOCATION:	Eternal Lawns Memorial Park – Business Office
TIME:	Early Morning
SYNOPSIS:	Martin has come to the Memorial Park business office to arrange for his father's funeral.
GENRE:	Comedy

(Martin enters carrying a paper grocery bag and sits quietly. A moment later DAMON RAVEN – Client Representative with a file folder.)

                        RAVEN
Mr. Nelson? Mr. Martin Nelson?

                        MARTIN
Yes… you can all me Martin.

                    RAVEN
Sorry to keep you waiting... it's been a very busy morning.

                    MARTIN
It's not even eight o'clock...

                    RAVEN
Mornings are our busy time... and this morning's decedent traffic is heavier than normal...

   (Tries to make a joke)

People are just dying to get in here

                    MARTIN
I guess.

                    RAVEN
I'm Damon Raven Client Representative... and on behalf of Eternal Lawns Memorial Park... I want to extend my condolences for the loss of your mother.

                    MARTIN
Father... his name was John Nelson.

                    RAVEN
Father... and want you to rest assured that all the members of our memorial park staff are here to guide you during this time of need.

                    MARTIN
Thank you.

   (Raven opens the file.)

                    RAVEN
Now, it seems that we have all the required information already in this file... it says here that your father had taken advantage of our **Forethought Memorial Plan**, which means that his funeral has already been planned and paid for.

MARTIN
He was a very organized man... liked to leave no stone unturned.

RAVEN
A wonderful quality... and may I say... very thoughtful to pre plan... now it says here... that you... Mr. Martin.

MARTIN
My father...

RAVEN
Your father had purchased a **"Basic" Harmony package**... that entitles him to the basic funeral services and of course internment in our memorial park.

MARTIN
That's my understanding... are we missing anything?

RAVEN
Well... the basic plan includes just what it says... the "basic" amenities and services.

MARTIN
...and those are?

(Raven flips the folder around toward Martin.)

RAVEN
Casket... basic Gainesboro grey or rustic bronze faux finish... burial within **The Wall of Remembrance** and appropriate grave marker printed in Cambria type face with a standard salutation not to exceed 20 characters (including spaces) and of course the decedent's name.

MARTIN
Standard salutation?

RAVEN
Something like "In Loving Memory... that's sixteen characters... decedent's name would appear under that... no character limitation... full birth and death dates are extra.

MARTIN
I have no experience at this… are twenty characters enough?

RAVEN
Mr. Nelson… when someone you love has passed, you may wonder, where do I start? What do I do? That's why I'm here… to guide you through your loss.

MARTIN
Thank you.

RAVEN
You are welcome… Mr. Nelson… by the way… what is your vocation?

MARTIN
I teach history… at the community college.

RAVEN
How nice… history is so much part of who we are… and what we will become and ultimately what legacy we leave after we are gone. I'm thinking of the Ancient Egyptians Mr. Nelson… they left us an amazing legacy. Wouldn't you say?

MARTIN
I guess… I teach American History.

RAVEN
American history…and for that very reason… an educated person such as yourself understands the need to arrange all funeral plans at one time, with one understanding counselor. If the battle of Gettysburg has taught us anything… it points to those dearly departed souls interred on that "hallowed" ground… one special place… serving as mortuary, crematory, church, cemetery, mausoleum, and flower shop all in one, with funeral processions conducted within the confines a beautiful memorial-park.

(Beat.)

Unfortunately... the basic Harmony package doesn't have any of these enhancements.

MARTIN
I see... how would I get those extra things for my dad?

RAVEN
I'm so glad you asked Mr. Nelson... we have several other packages that would include some of the amenities I've mentioned but the best value for your investment would be our top of the line **Elegance package**.

MARTIN
Elegance? How much is that?

RAVEN
Now let's not just look at price... let's look at value. **The Elegance Package** includes a full couch Princeton Copper casket... burial in the Garden Meadow... overlooking San Fernando Valley... premium polystyrene concrete grave liner, raised grave marker with unlimited century gothic inscription, full funeral services including custom written eulogy by a licensed non denominational clergyman and a **spectacular** free-standing flower arrangement.

MARTIN
Spectacular?

RAVEN
Yes... our **Deepest Sympathies Standing Spray – White** is the most popular.

White flowers are often sought after as symbols of honor, reverence and remembrance. This striking standing spray—exquisitely crafted by our expert memorial park floral team from an assortment of pure white blooms is the perfect expression of all the love, compassion and support you feel during your time of mourning... and at no additional cost... we will play a pre recorded version of **Amazing Grace** at grave site. With the

Elegance Package you get all of these amenities for the value price of only twenty one thousand dollars.

                        MARTIN

Wow! Twenty-one grand! That's way over anything I can afford.

                        RAVEN

I didn't tell you the good part yet...

                        MARTIN

What's that?

                        RAVEN

You're entitled to a casket discount of $4200... which takes it down to let's see...

    (Raven scribbles some numbers in his file.)

That's twenty one thousand minus forty two hundred... that gets us down to Sixteen Thousand Eight Hundred out the door.

                        MARTIN

What about the basic package... I think my father paid $7,500 for that... isn't there a credit for that?

    (Beat.)

                        RAVEN

You drive a hard bargain Mr. Nelson... we don't usually do this... but let me talk to my manager and see what I can do for you. But before I go in there and fight for you... and the remembrance of John Nelson... I want to ask... are you ready to make this purchase today?

                        MARTIN

Yes... if the price is something I can afford.

                        RAVEN

I can tell that you are a wonderful teacher... very smart and you drive a hard bargain.

(RAVEN exits as Martin sits quietly... then springs back in again and sits. Before he speaks, he adds some numbers in his file.)

Okay... Okay... let me just add this up. It was tough Mr. Nelson... very tough but I fought hard for you and got my manager to go down to fifteen thousand... as long as we do this today.

MARTIN
What other day am I going to do it? My father is here already.

RAVEN
Good. I glad you feel this way... so where are we? I can put you in the Elegance Package... loaded with all the extras including the Princeton Copper Casket... I'm talking top of the line.... all for 15K out the door!

MARTIN
I don't know?

RAVEN
15K for the the memory of your dear father?

MARTIN
I'm just not sure... do we really need a copper casket?

RAVEN
No comparison with the faux bronze. Would you like to see the Princeton Copper Casket? I have one in the back... once you see it, feel the quality of the interior... you're going to love it! This is a 32 oz. Copper totally loaded with locking mechanism and GPS in a light brown brushed copper finish exterior, champagne velvet interior or if you don't like brown, I can get you one from another mortuary in a taupe brushed finish exterior with pink velvet interior. Brand new... I can have it here by this afternoon.

MARTIN
Let me think about it...

RAVEN
The casket deal is only good for today... by tomorrow someone else is going to roll in here and get it... then it's gone. If money is an issue... I can

set you up with our finance people... and do a payment plan. So what do you say?

(Beat.)

MARTIN

Let's just go with the basic package... the one my father bought.

(Beat.)

RAVEN

Okay, no problem... if it's his wish... then it's his wish...

MARTIN

Thank you... is it possible to put an article in the casket with him?

RAVEN

Not a problem.

(Martin hands him the paper bag and Raven looks into it.)

RAVEN

This is a pair of sneakers? You want these placed in his casket?

MARTIN

Those were his favorite shoes... he was a runner. He wore them all the time until he... well he couldn't walk any more. I figure where's he's going in Heaven... he can use them again.

(Raven starts to write, then gets tears in his eyes and puts his pen down.)

RAVEN

Mr. Nelson, that's the most loving thing I have ever heard anyone say while doing this job... it's a **beautiful** gesture.

MARTIN

Thank you...

                    RAVEN
It's such a beautiful gesture... I tell you what I'm gonna do...because I just know you are a caring and wonderful son to your father. I am going get you the Elegance package for $14K... can you do 14K? You can put those running sneakers in a 32 inch Princeton Copper Casket... what do you say?

   (Martin thinks a moment, then smiles.)

                    MARTIN
Okay... I'll do it... for my dad.

                    RAVEN

For your dad... now do you want to go with the brown or should I get you the taupe?

                    MARTIN
...I'll go with the brown...

                    RAVEN
An excellent choice Mr. Martin... excellent choice.

#21 CHE CHE – The Song
Adapted from the screenplay Che Che

GENDER: (Male/Female)

AGE RANGE: Adult (30's – 40's)

CHARACTERS: **CHE CHE** – (30's – 40's) a paradox of a man caught somewhere between heaven and earth, an former New York Mafia hit man now hiding in Sicily. He's dusty, disheveled and darkened by the Sicilian sun and lives in a small cottage on a mountaintop overlooking the Mediterranean Sea.

MARA – (late 20's) a famous American pop singer on her way down.

She is living on the edge of extinction. Sleepless nights, drugs and alcohol consume her world.

LOCATION: A small cottage in Sicily overlooking the Mediterranean Sea.

TIME: Early Morning

SYNOPSIS: A fading pop singer recording her comeback album in a remote Sicilian castle meets a New York mafia hit man in hiding. Che Che rescues Mara, after she's had too much to drink and has fallen down a small cliff during an intense thunderstorm. He takes her to his cottage for the night. It is now morning and she is singing with an acoustic guitar. She sings sadly but with a beauty Che Che has never seen before.

GENRE: Drama

#21 CHE CHE – The Song

(Mara plays a sad song on Che Che's acoustic guitar and sings as he enters with fresh basil from his garden. The storm is gone and the sun breaking through the clouds has made the air warm and sweet.)

*Note: Mara can sing a small portion of any song acapella if no instrumentation is available.

CHE CHE
Nice song... but very sad... did you write it?

MARA
I did... you speak English?

CHE CHE
Yeah... everyone keeps asking me that.

MARA
Well... we **are** in Sicily.

CHE CHE
You sleep okay?

MARA
I think so.

CHE CHE
You slept right through the thunder...

MARA
I had no choice... too much Bourbon and pills.

CHE CHE
You gotta stay away from that stuff.

MARA
That stuff has got to stay away from me...

(She falters when she tries to walk then he gets up and helps her.)

CHE CHE
Take it easy... you had a pretty big fall.

MARA
You know I should thank you... do you know who I am?

CHE CHE
No... am I supposed to?

MARA
You don't know that I'm a famous singer?

CHE CHE
Well... we are in Sicily.

MARA
I can't believe that you've never heard me sing.

CHE CHE
I just heard you now.

MARA
Guess you don't have much internet here...

CHE CHE
No... that's the beauty of this place.

MARA
Okay, let's start all over.... my name is Mara. And you?

CHE CHE
My name is Che Che... Frank in American... you can call me Frank.

MARA
No... I like Che Che...

CHE CHE
Okay, then.

MARA
Did you put this shirt on me?

CHE CHE
Your clothes were soaked from the rain... I couldn't let you stay all night in wet clothes... so I took them off and put on the shirt.

MARA
Really?

CHE CHE
Don't worry... I didn't look.

MARA
Thanks...

CHE CHE
For not looking?

MARA
...and for helping.

CHE CHE
You're welcome... you want some coffee?

MARA
That would be great...

#22 CHE CHE – Coffee
Adapted from the screenplay Che Che

GENDER: (Male/Female)

AGE RANGE: Adult (30's – 40's)

CHARACTERS: **CHE CHE** – (30's – 40's) a paradox of a man caught somewhere between heaven and earth, a former New York Mafia hit man now hiding in Sicily. He's dusty, disheveled and darkened by the Sicilian sun and lives in a small cottage on a mountaintop overlooking the Mediterranean Sea.

MARA – (late 20's) a famous American pop singer on her way down.

She is living on the edge of extinction. Sleepless nights, drugs and alcohol consume her existence.

LOCATION: A small cottage in Sicily overlooking the Mediterranean Sea.

TIME: Early Morning

SYNOPSIS: A fading pop singer recording her comeback album in a remote Sicilian castle meets a New York mafia hit man in hiding. Che Che reveals to Mara that he is quite more than just a simple man living in the hills of Sicily.

GENRE: Drama

#22 CHE CHE – Coffee

(Mara sips a delicate little cup of coffee as she looks at the large collection of books that surround the cottage walls.)

MARA

This is really strong coffee…

CHE CHE

You don't like it?

MARA

No, I love it this way.

CHE CHE

Me too.

MARA

Italian?

CHE CHE

Me? Yes…

MARA

And the coffee?

CHE CHE

Persian. I lived with a Persian family when I first came here… I learned how to make coffee from them.

(She smiles)

What is it?

MARA

Funny…

CHE CHE

What?

MARA
This place of yours is actually very nice... all these books... the vegetable garden... the Persian coffee in these fine little cups. Looking at you, I wouldn't have thought... you'd be this way.

CHE CHE
You mean my shirt? That's just soil from my garden... I can put on a clean one.

MARA
No... you're fine... you just look...

CHE CHE
Like a homeless guy?

MARA
No of course not... let's just say you look "rustic."

CHE CHE
I've been called a lot of things in my life... but never rustic.

MARA
You know... "of the earth." Earthy.

CHE CHE
Okay, that's not so bad... but I still will clean up a bit and put on a new shirt.

(He pours her some more coffee and then disappears behind a curtain.)

MARA
Are all the books on these walls yours?

(Che Che from behind the curtain.)

CHE CHE
Yeah...

MARA

Have you read them all?

CHE CHE

No... I just look at the pictures.

MARA

Very funny...

(He throws out his dirty shirt as she takes a book on the table and reads it aloud.)

"Heaven is what I cannot reach... the apple on the tree..."

(The pages are faded and she has trouble reading the next line when Che Che finishes it from behind the curtain.)

CHE CHE

"Provide it do hopeless hang,
That heaven is to me."

(Che Che appears from behind the curtain clean, hair combed back. Mara looks at him for the first time without dirt on face and likes what she sees.)

CHE CHE

"The color on the cruising cloud,
The interdicted ground...
Behind the hill, the house behind...
There Paradise is found."

(There is silence... Mara finally breaks it.)

MARA

You know it... every word.

CHE CHE

Emily Dickenson.

MARA
Who the hell are you?

CHE CHE
I told you... Che Che.

MARA
Che Che... do you know all of these books by heart?

CHE CHE
Just the ones that mean something to me...

MARA
You must read a lot then?

CHE CHE
I do... the reading habit was literally beat into me when I was a kid in school.

MARA
What kind of school did you go to?

CHE CHE
Catholic school... the nuns were very persuasive... they would whack you with a stick if you didn't listen... I didn't want to get whacked... so I listened.

MARA
Nobody likes getting whacked.

CHE CHE
Yeah... I guess so...

MARA
So, from New York to Sicily right?

CHE CHE
I never said anything about New York.

MARA
It was just a guess.

CHE CHE
I take the fifth...

MARA
Very funny... then answer this... why did you come here to live?

(He hesitates as he pours himself more coffee.)

CHE CHE
I killed a few people.

MARA
Oh?

CHE CHE
...and now a few people wanna kill me. More coffee?

MARA
I should be heading back.

CHE CHE
I'll walk with you.

(Mara gets up.)

MARA
I'd like that.

(Che Che signals her to go first and they both exit.)

#23 AUTUMN SWEET
Autumn 1989 – the first day – Sabrina, scrambled eggs and the letters
Adapted from the play Autumn Sweet

GENDER:	(Male/Female)
AGE RANGE:	Adult (30's – 70's)
CHARACTERS:	**VERONICA COLLETTI** – (30's – 40's) an attractive, brilliant and world famous artist whose creative juices have run dry. She's come home after many years for her mother's funeral and comes face to face with her abusive father.
	JOHN COLLETTI (50's – 70's) a large built, dark Othello like man who when he was younger was overpowering and moody. He was an artist painter who never made it. A dreamer who has waited a lifetime for something important to happen in his life. A dream that never came for him. He is now an old man.
LOCATION:	Veronica's childhood home – Northport, Long Island, New York – the kitchen.
TIME:	Morning
SYNOPSIS:	Veronica, who lives in Paris, has come home after many years for her mother's funeral. She walks into her childhood home for the first time since she ran away and comes face to face with her abusive father.
GENRE:	Drama

(John is sitting at the kitchen table having a cup of tea. Veronica enters carrying a small suitcase, looks over at him and turns to the audience.)

VERONICA

No matter where I live ... Long Island will always be my home. It's the place my heart goes when I dream. I become a child again... cut out paper oak leaves I made at school... stuck together... paste on my hands and under my gloves... smelling like a wet dog in a glue patch.

(She walks into the house.)

Home is the place we return to bury our dead and recount the living. To be with family that circle linked by blood and fire to reopen old wounds and inflict new with amazing precision.

(Beat)

My mother has passed away and I have come back home to honor her... and to remember.

(Veronica turns to scene and enters. She and John look at each other in silence then she speaks.)

VERONICA

Hello...

JOHN

Hello Veronica...

VERONICA

Hello...

JOHN

You have a French accent?

VERONICA

I do?

JOHN
Well… just a little.

(Veronica and John have a polite but awkward embrace.)

I've been expecting you.

VERONICA
I've just come from the cemetery.

JOHN
I missed you at the funeral.

VERONICA
I had a delay getting a flight out of Paris… some sort of security scare.

(She searches for a word in English.)

How do you say?

JOHN
Shut down.

VERONICA
Yes…. it turned out to be nothing.

JOHN
The important thing is that you are here now.

(He pours more tea for himself.)

You look French too…

VERONICA
Should I say "thank you."

JOHN
Like Audrey Hepburn in the movie **"Sabrina."** You're real thin like her too.

VERONICA

...and you're not as tall as I remembered.

JOHN

I probably shrunk a little... Long Island weather will do that to you... it's the dampness.

   (Beat.)

You want something to eat? Here, I'll make you something... you must be starving after being on a plane so long.

VERONICA

No thank you... I'm fine.

   (John slowly rises, buttons his old tattered sweater and puts Mary's (Veronica's mother) apron over it.)

JOHN

When your mother got sick, I learned how to cook... can you imagine that? Not everything, just the basics... you want some eggs? I can do that.

VERONICA

How long was she ill?

JOHN

It's hard to tell... she kept it to herself for a long time. I didn't find out until almost the end. There was not much the doctors could do.

VERONICA

Why wasn't I told?

JOHN

Veronica... I hope you haven't come here to fight?

VERONICA

Why?

JOHN
She didn't want you to know... it was her wish... as far as "why?" She never told me.

VERONICA
Didn't she get my letters?

(John takes out a shoebox and puts it on the table.)

JOHN
There all here... she must have read them a million times.

VERONICA
Why didn't she write back?

(Beat.)

JOHN
She did... those letters are in the box too. She never sent them.

VERONICA
Why?

JOHN
I think she was embarrassed of her writing... she wanted it just perfect.

(Beat.)

She even took a poetry class at the community college... I'll show you... but I got to get my glasses.

(John gets up.)

VERONICA
Where are you going?

JOHN
Upstairs to get my glasses... I can't read a damn thing anymore without them.

> (Beat.)

It's good to have you home.

> (John exits. As he does, Veronica opens the box and takes out one of the letters and reads.)

VERONICA

Dear Veronica, I hope you are living a wonderful life in Paris… I miss you more than you know… and think of you often when you were a little girl… you remind me so much of my own grandmother… full of life! You remember the story I told you about your grandmother? She was seventeen when she sailed to this country on the bottom of an overcrowded steam ship. She was just an Italian farm girl who left her quiet village in Italy to marry a man she had never met before.

When her ship sailed into New York harbor, she came up on the ship's deck for the first time and saw the dark smoke coming from the stacks of all the factories filling the sky with a blackness that blocked out the sun. She cried out in Italian: **"El cielo stu forgo!"… The sky is on fire…** she thought the sky in America was on fire… do you remember that story? If you're reading this… it means that I'm gone… please forgive me for not telling you about my cancer. I didn't want you to worry about me. Also I want you to try to forgive your father… he's changed more than you know. Love Mom.

> (Veronica stops reading… looks up to see that John has returned and is standing in the doorway looking at her.)

#24 AUTUMN SWEET
Autumn 1989 – the second day – chiaroscuro, Lipton Tea, and the paint box
Adapted from the play Autumn Sweet

GENDER: (Male/Female)

AGE RANGE: Adult (30's – 70's)

CHARACTERS: **VERONICA COLLETTI** – (30's – 40's) an attractive, brilliant and world famous artist whose creative juices have run dry. She has come home after many years to attend her mother's funeral and comes face to face with her abusive father.

JOHN COLLETTI (50's – 70's) a large built, dark Othello like man who when he was younger was overpowering and moody.

He was an artist painter who never made it. A dreamer who has waited a lifetime for something important to happen in his life.

A dream that never came for him. He is now an old man.

LOCATION: Veronica's childhood home – Northport, Long Island, New York – the kitchen.

TIME: Late Afternoon – autumn 1989

SYNOPSIS: Veronica, who lives in Paris, has come home after many years for her mother's funeral. She walks into her childhood home for the first time since she ran away and comes face to face with her abusive father. Veronica confronts her father for the first time and learns the truth about her past.

GENRE: Drama

(Veronica is at the kitchen table, with an open shoebox of her mother's unsent letters next to her. She rips open an unopened letter.)

VERONICA

October 31st 1966... Dear Mom... why haven't you written back to me? Please write back even if it's a short note. School at the Sorbonne is wonderful. I'm learning about a new technique called chiaroscuro... a method of rendering light and shade... and then I remembered something...

(Beat)

Dad standing over my shoulder for hours showing me how to paint the subtle variations of light and shade... he was the one that taught me that.

(John enters)

JOHN

Been catching up on your reading?

VERONICA

I don't think I'll ever catch up... I should put these all back and quit while I'm ahead.

JOHN

Just think of all the money I saved on postage.

(Veronica doesn't laugh at his joke.)

You want a cup of tea?

VERONICA
I don't think so.

JOHN
I can brew a whole pot... it's Lipton.

VERONICA
I hate Lipton tea.

JOHN
Why, no Lipton tea in Paris?

VERONICA
No.

JOHN
Why am I not surprised... okay, so don't have tea.

VERONICA
I'm sorry about this morning... I didn't come here to fight with you.

JOHN
There's no blood on the floor... so I guess we're doing okay.

VERONICA
You were right when you said that we are all that's left of this family. It's just the two of us.

JOHN
"Family." I'm beginning to hate that word. It's just a convenient grouping of people to have around as prey... to hunt down and kill... during the holidays.

VERONICA
That's all... what about love?

JOHN
Love makes it worse.... the deeper the love... the stronger the venom.

VERONICA
The years have made you more articulate… but you're still full of hate. But I'm going to stop now… because I don't want to fight again.

JOHN
No fight… I'm not full of hate… what I'm talking about is pure science. It's all about our genetic makeup… that's why we act the way we do…. I read it in National Geographic.

(Beat.)

You sure you don't want any tea?

(She shakes her head "no.")

All our little so-called idiosyncrasies are passed on to us through our genes. My father passed them on to me and I passed them on to you… it's normal.

VERONICA
I'm not like you at all.

JOHN
I'm sorry to break this to you… but **yes** you are… the pattern has been set.

VERONICA
A pattern can be broken.

JOHN
Not this one.

VERONICA
Especially this one! I will never forget what you did to me!

JOHN
Right! Never forget! What do you want to do put me on a cross? Is that what it will take to make it right for you?

(Beat.)

No answer? Or is it because you like playing the martyr... the poor abused little girl!

VERONICA
Stop... that's quite enough!

JOHN
You just don't get it... this **"thing"** you're so upset about is all part of being a family. We all do things to one another that we don't want to do... but somehow they happen... and sometimes we do really bad things... all we can say is "I'm sorry..." Then kiss each other on the cheek and try to make it all okay... that is until the next time... when we do it all again. The pattern is set for eternity.

VERONICA
I think it's time for me to go.

JOHN
Then go... you haven't been home for twenty years... you think it makes a difference? Well let me tell you... it doesn't. So be my guest... go!

VERONICA
I'm wasting my time trying to talk to you.

    (Beat)

JOHN
Yes you are... and what the hell did I do to you that was so bad?

    (She doesn't answer.)

I'll tell you... I taught you how to paint... yeah you went to that fancy Sorbonne school... but what ever it is that made you what you are... I put it there!

And don't you ever forget it!

    (Veronica starts to walk out.)

Where you going?

VERONICA
Upstairs to pack.

JOHN
Great back to Paris... and your famous life... I just want to give you something... this was **my** paint box... now I'm giving it to you. Take it.

(He gives her a small box of paints and brushes.)

VERONICA
This is it? The things that made me famous... these dried up old tubes of paint and worn brushes? When I was a little girl, you forced me to use... these.... all I ever wanted to do was play with my dolls like a normal child... but you forced me day after day to paint... Paint again and again until I could hardly stand. Then you got jealous because I was too good... better than you.

JOHN
I taught you everything... Everything I knew...

VERONICA
You make yourself sound so noble. The **great** teacher... all you were was a hack... a five-dollar a portrait hack!

JOHN
Then I guess you're a hack... because I created you just like a canvass... I sketched you and then filled you in line by line... without me... you wouldn't be a painter... without me... there'd be no Autumn Sweet.

VERONICA
That painting was all my idea... I painted it on my own.

JOHN
I painted it first!

VERONICA
You're a liar!

JOHN

No... I described it to you line by line... over and over again... every detail... every color... every line... you were just a little girl but my painting became your masterpiece... it got you into the Sorbonne... and changed your life.

VERONICA

You gave me nothing... all you did was take that wooden box and break my hands in it... do you remember that? I was only a child... when you put my hands in the box and crushed them?

(John turns away.)

Here, take a look! The scars you made are still there! They had to put me back together like a piece of shattered glass... you tried to break me... your jealousy only made me stronger. Thank you for that

JOHN

I'm so sorry...

VERONICA

No, I'm so sorry... sorry for you. Now if you'll excuse me, I need to go upstairs and pack.

(Veronica turns to leave... John watches her silently then speaks quietly.)

JOHN

Wait... please.

(Veronica stops and turns toward him.)

Please, don't leave... not now not this way... once you walk out that door, I know I will never see you again. I need more time... I need more time to make you see... to make your understand.

(Beat.)

Please, stay one more day... for mom.

(In silence, Veronica and John really look at each other for the first time.)

VERONICA
Okay... one more day... for mom.

(She exits. John remains with tears in his eyes.)

JOHN
For mom...

#25 THE SIGHTING

GENDER:	(Male/Female)
AGE RANGE:	Adult (30's)
CHARACTERS:	**DR. JONES** – (30's) a trauma care doctor at an emergency room at a local hospital just outside of Kecksburg, Pennsylvania.
	REGINA TAYLOR (20's – 30's) a newly wed married to David Taylor an advertising executive from New York City.
LOCATION:	A small ER interview room in a small town just outside of Kecksburg, Pennsylvania
TIME:	Late evening - December 9, 1965
SYNOPSIS:	Regina and her husband decided drive to her parents home in Pittsburgh when a bright light in the sky gets their attention.
GENRE:	Drama

(Regina Lane sits at a table with her eyes closed in a small ER waiting room. SOUND of the Byrd's **"Turn Turn Turn"** plays in her head. The music stops abruptly when Dr. Jones, in a white lab coat, enters.)

*Note – Regina can also hum or sing song acapella if using the recording is not possible.

DR. JONES
Mrs. Taylor?

REGINA
Yes?

DR. JONES
I apologize for the long wait...

REGINA
It's three in the morning.

DR. JONES
I realize that.

REGINA
When can I see my husband?

DR. JONES
He's sedated right now... maybe in the morning. Right now I would like to ask you a few questions so I can get a better understanding of what happened.

REGINA
Doctor Jones... I've been sitting here over four hours. What kind of place is this? There's not even a candy machine or water fountain in the hallway.

DR. JONES
I'm sorry... I am not...

(She cuts him off.)

REGINA
Maybe just a cup of water... that would help.

DR. JONES
If we could communicate just for a few moments?

REGINA
I want to see my husband... I should also call my parents... if I can use the phone... or if there's a pay phone anywhere? Can someone change a dollar bill?

(Beat. He sits down across from her.)

DR. JONES
I am assigned to you now and need you to tell me what happened. What exactly did you see?

REGINA
We were driving... to my parent's house in Pittsburgh... it's our anniversary tomorrow... December 10th, 1965... married one year! We were taking a one of those country roads... off the turnpike... no traffic and making great time... the road was narrow with woods on either side of us... but it was empty... and we had the music blasting on the radio.

DR. JONES
What about atmospheric effects?

REGINA
Weather?

DR. JONES
Yes...

REGINA
A typical winter day... cloudy and cold all the way... but no snow.

DR. JONES
How long had you been driving your vehicle?

REGINA
From New York?

DR. JONES
No, since your last recharge.

REGINA
Gas stop? Maybe three or four hours...

DR. JONES
Any feelings of fatigue?

REGINA
What difference would that make?

DR. JONES
I'm just trying to evaluate your state. Then, if you can summarize what happened next?

REGINA
Suddenly the sky lit up... there was a large fireball that flew very low right over us. We felt the ground shake and then there was a large sonic boom... like a jet plane... I felt it in my ears.

DR. JONES
You both saw this?

REGINA
Yes.

DR. JONES
So it was just a fireball?

REGINA
No... it had a definite shape.

DR. JONES
What kind of shape?

(Beat. She thinks for moment.)

REGINA
A bell... it looked just like a bell... and had some sort of markings on it.

DR. REGINA
You saw writing?

REGINA
A symbol... like I said... it flew very low... right over us...

DR. JONES
What kind of symbol?

(Beat.)

REGINA
This will sound strange... but it looked like a German eagle... with a swastika on it... but that couldn't be possible.

DR. JONES
How do you know it was a German eagle?"

REGINA
Eagles have wings... it was an eagle with its wings spread out. Aren't you going to write this all down?

DR. JONES
What happened then?

REGINA
We kept driving toward a glow in the sky... and turned the radio.

DR. JONES
Why did you do that?

REGINA
To try to hear what was going on... we thought it could have been a Russian attack.

DR. JONES
The Russians?

REGINA
Yes... a missile attack. Don't you read the newspapers?

DR. JONES
I'm sorry... what did you hear on the radio?

(She tries to recall folds her head into her hands.)

REGINA

Just static... and then there was that song... *To everything (turn, turn, turn) There is a season (turn, turn, turn) - And a time to every purpose, under heaven.* The same song was playing on all the stations. Now I keep hearing it...

DR. JONES

You still hear it?

REGINA

In my head... I keep hearing it my head.

DR. JONES

What happened then?

REGINA

We kept following the glow in the sky... then there was a hot bright flash... it was silent but you could feel the heat on your face... and then everything went black...

DR. JONES

You passed out?

REGINA

No... different... an endless blackness... I felt like I was floating.

DR. JONES

After that?

REGINA

I opened my eyes... it was nighttime and there was a crystal clear sky over our heads... the glow in the sky was gone and I could see the stars... but it was summer time... the trees were greener... and I could hear crickets... lots of crickets... are there a lot of crickets in this part of Pennsylvania?

DR. JONES

What was the next event?

REGINA
Then I realized that our car was parked at the side of the road. I couldn't move... then I looked over at David in the driver's seat. He looked like he'd been taken apart and put back together again.

DR. JONES
Did he speak?

REGINA
His mouth moved... but no sound came out. It was terrible. Then there were headlights a car... coming towards us... The next thing I remember is waking up in this room with my head on this table. That's it.

DR. JONES
Have you left anything out?

REGINA
One more thing ... I don't remember the car having a driver.

(SOUND – A RING TONE coming from inside Jones's jacket.)

REGINA
What's that sound?

DR. JONES
Nothing you need to worry about. Thank you Mrs. Taylor.

(Dr. Jones stands and speaks as if he is communicating with someone.)

DR. JONES
Time vortex confirmed... approximately one hundred years... 1966 to 2066.

(Then in German.)

Die Glocke ist angekommen (the bell has arrived.)

REGINA
What the heck is a time vortex? What's **die glocke?**

DR. JONES

Mrs. Taylor... please remain here.

REGINA

Where is here?

DR. JONES

I am not programed to answer that... please remain. Thank you.

REGINA

Not programmed? What does that mean?

DR. JONES

Thank you... Mrs. Taylor.

    (Dr. Jones exits.)

REGINA

Dr. Jones! Where am I? I want to see my husband! Where is my husband?

Is there anybody here? Anyone? Hello!

    (Beat. she sits back down again.)

I'm so tired. So tired.

    (She sits back in the chair, closes her eyes and puts her head down on the table.)

    (SOUND – Static – then the song... *To everything (turn, turn, turn) There is a season (turn, turn, turn) - And a time to every purpose, under heaven.*)

Alternate – Regina can sing the song to herself aloud.

Made in the USA
Columbia, SC
21 August 2024